NEW DIRECTIONS FOR INSTITUTIONAL RESEARCH

Patrick T. Terenzini
The Pennsylvania State University
EDITOR-IN-CHIEF

Ellen Earle Chaffee
North Dakota Board of Higher Education
ASSOCIATE EDITOR

Evaluating Student Recruitment and Retention Programs

Don Hossler
Indiana University

EDITOR

Number 70, Summer 1991

JOSSEY-BASS INC., PUBLISHERS, San Francisco

MAXWELL MACMILLAN INTERNATIONAL PUBLISHING GROUP
New York • Oxford • Singapore • Sydney • Toronto

EVALUATING STUDENT RECRUITMENT AND RETENTION PROGRAMS
Don Hossler (ed.)
New Directions for Institutional Research, no. 70
Volume XVIII, Number 2
Patrick T. Terenzini, Editor-in-Chief
Ellen Earle Chaffee, Associate Editor

LC 85-645339   ISSN 0271-0579   ISBN 1-55542-792-8

NEW DIRECTIONS FOR INSTITUTIONAL RESEARCH is part of The Jossey-Bass Adult and Higher Education Series and is published quarterly by Jossey-Bass Inc., Publishers (publication number USPS 098-830). Second-class postage paid at San Francisco, California, and at additional mailing offices. Postmaster: Send address changes to Jossey-Bass Inc., Publishers, 350 Sansome Street, San Francisco, California 94104.

EDITORIAL CORRESPONDENCE should be sent to the Editor-in-Chief, Patrick T. Terenzini, Center for the Study of Higher Education, The Pennsylvania State University, 403 South Allen Street, Suite 104, University Park, Pennsylvania 16801-5202.

Photograph of the library by Michael Graves at San Juan Capistrano by Chad Slattery © 1984. All rights reserved.

Printed on acid-free paper in the United States of America.

356522

CONTENTS

EDITOR'S NOTES   1
Don Hossler

1. Setting the Context for Evaluation of Recruitment and   5
Retention Programs
Michael G. Dolence
Effective evaluation of recruitment and retention programs is based on set-
ting clear goals, asking the right questions, and establishing a context for
interpretation of the results.

2. Creating an Environment in Which Evaluation-Oriented   21
Student Information Systems Can Successfully Compete for
Resources
Anthony Lolli
Effective use of student information systems for evaluation requires collab-
oration among an array of campus administrators.

3. Evaluating the Impact of Institutional Contacts   33
Marian F. Pagano, Dawn Geronimo Terkla
Annual assessments of student recruitment contacts can lead to more effec-
tive recruitment strategies.

4. Evaluating the Impact of Financial Aid on Student Recruitment   47
and Retention
Lee Wilcox
An analysis of the impact of financial aid on recruitment and retention can
help guide financial aid policies.

5. Tracking Academic Progress Within a Complex Academic   61
Environment
Richard D. Howard, Brenda H. Rogers
Methods of evaluating student retention and graduation rates at complex
universities are examined.

6. Evaluating Retention-Driven Marketing in a Community College: 73
An Alternative Approach
Richard Tichenor, John J. Cosgrove
Evaluation can be used to develop retention-driven marketing strategies
directed toward encouraging students to re-enroll.

7. Monitoring Shifts in Campus Image and Recruitment Efforts in   83
Small Colleges
David Murray
The monitoring of institutional trend data and data from comparable insti-
tutions is a useful evaluation tool for determining the effectiveness of recruit-
ment and retention activities.

8. Evaluating Recruitment and Retention Programs   95
Don Hossler
Ongoing evaluation of recruitment and retention programs must be grounded
in the context of academic programs and policies.

INDEX   101

EDITOR'S NOTES

College and university administrators have been concerned about student enrollments for more than a decade. The attention directed at enrollments is attributable to several factors, including a declining pool of high school graduates, external demands for improvements in student persistence rates as one measure of institutional effectiveness, and enrollment goals that target special student populations (minority students, talented students, and so on). As a result an array of new recruitment and retention programs has been implemented.

The cost of recruiting and retaining students has risen dramatically during the past few years. Hard figures are difficult to find because the costs of recruitment and retention programs can be spread across a number of budgetary units, including academic units, admissions, financial aid, public relations, and student affairs. Nevertheless, many financial analysts have suggested that growth in admissions, financial aid, and student affairs units partially explains the rising costs of higher education during the 1980s. It is surprising that despite the increase in institutional resources directed at recruitment and retention programs, little information on the evaluation of these programs has found its way into print.

This volume, *Evaluating Student Recruitment and Retention Programs,* will help fill this gap. Moreover, it is designed to stimulate additional work in the areas. Examples from major public and private universities, a private liberal arts college, and a community college are included. The chapters were selected to represent a range of evaluation activities in these areas, from the standpoints of the impact of financial aid on both areas, to the major sectors of higher education, to the diverse evaluation techniques and concerns at major public and private universities, a private liberal arts college, and a community college.

In Chapter One, Michael G. Dolence provides an overview of the issues related to the evaluation of recruitment and retention programs. Dolence suggests that formative evaluation should be the primary approach to these programs. He also advocates linking strategic planning to evaluation activities, since in the absence of clearly articulated goals for recruitment and retention it is impossible to evaluate the effectiveness of recruitment and retention programs. In closing, he shares practical insights into what can be learned through evaluation.

Anthony Lolli, in Chapter Two, argues that student information systems are the foundation of effective evaluation of recruitment and retention programs. Lolli points out that many campus administrators overlook the hard decisions that must be made in order to facilitate evaluation activities. He notes that hardware and software must be designed by collaborative groups of institutional researchers and campus administrators if evaluation results are to be useful to a diverse array of users. Furthermore, Lolli wisely points out that few campuses can afford to collect and store every conceivably useful datum. Thus, evaluators must realistically assess the importance of information and choose only those data that have consistently practical value.

Marian F. Pagano and Dawn Geronimo Terkla provide a primer on how to conduct evaluation studies of recruitment activities. In Chapter Three, they describe a set of instruments and survey questions used at Tufts University to conduct an ongoing series of evaluations. The authors indicate how the results from these evaluations have been used to shape institutional recruitment activities.

In Chapter Four, Lee Wilcox discusses the evaluation of student financial aid in student recruitment and retention. Using examples from Rensselaer Polytechnic Institute, Wilcox describes techniques that have been used to evaluate the impact of increased student financial aid on recruitment of new freshmen. In addition, he outlines an evaluation study used to assess the impact of aid on student persistence rates. In both instances he explains how these evaluation studies were used to shape financial aid policy at Rensselaer.

Chapter Five discusses methods for evaluating student retention at medium-sized to large universities. Drawing on their experiences at North Carolina State University, Richard D. Howard and Brenda H. Rogers analyze issues in data base development and management. They identify key variables that should be tracked in a longitudinal data base and suggest how data should be interpreted. Howard and Rogers also include examples of how retention evaluation studies have been used to guide institutional policy making.

In Chapter Six, Richard Tichenor and John J. Cosgrove describe how the multi-campus system of Saint Louis Community College has used evaluation studies to develop enrollment strategies that can be viewed as both retention and marketing activities. The authors first describe what Saint Louis Community College has learned about why students do not re-enroll. Using the insights gained from this knowledge, Tichenor and Cosgrove go on to describe a series of marketing initiatives to motivate these nonreturning students to re-enroll. They also share their techniques for evaluating the effectiveness of these marketing initiatives.

In Chapter Seven, David Murray presents an overview of a series of recruitment and retention activities at DePauw University. He also discusses how these activities are evaluated. DePauw is a small liberal arts college that frequently uses trend data and comparisons with similar institutions in order to evaluate the effectiveness of new programs. Murray also discusses a new approach to marketing that has the potential to significantly change mail-marketing strategies at colleges and universities and how DePauw is evaluating the success of this new approach.

In Chapter Eight, I describe the limits of evaluation, noting that the changing nature of recruitment activities and financial aid awards can quickly date the findings of evaluation studies. The chapter asserts that evaluative information must be grounded in the context of institutional events and enrollment trends at other institutions. The apparent success or failure of recruitment and retention programs may be the result of events outside of the control of campus administrators. Nevertheless, I conclude that evaluation activities are necessary if institutions are to spend scarce resources wisely.

Don Hossler
Editor

Don Hossler is associate professor and chair of the Department of Educational Leadership and Policy Studies in the School of Education, Indiana University, Bloomington.

The maintenance of effective recruitment and retention programs is an institutionwide concern. To maintain institutional health and vitality, meaningful evaluation of recruitment and retention is necessary.

Setting the Context for Evaluation of Recruitment and Retention Programs

Michael G. Dolence

Evaluation is a natural part of effective management. Evaluation is as much an art as a science, often relying on insight and intuition as well as on the rigors of statistical analysis. While in its purest form evaluation is conducted without bias or prejudice, the realities of human nature make absolute objectivity in this endeavor nearly impossible. The exact nature of an evaluation depends largely on the intent of the investigators, even though the intent may never be specified by the investigators to campus administrators. The intent or perceived intent establishes the tone of an evaluation and can have a significant impact on its quality and usefulness. Effective program evaluation also requires the cooperation and assistance of those being evaluated. A well-designed process takes into account that evaluation involves people and thus provides appropriate means of communication among participants to facilitate input, review findings, and suggest alternatives.

The basic purposes of program evaluation are to judge the worth or value of a program, to assist in policy decisions, and to provide information to support or refute political decisions (Talmage, 1982). Program evaluation can fulfill these purposes by addressing five classic questions: (1) Is this program any good? (2) What is it good for? (3) Is it better than something else? (4) Can I make it better? (5) Is it appropriate for the policy objective? (Gowen and Green, 1980). An understanding of the concept of value is key to answering these questions.

Determination of a program's value is a subjective process, which can be examined from three different perspectives. The *societal-political-economic* perspective assesses value in terms of a program's impact on people. The

New Directions for Institutional Research, no. 70, Summer 1991 © Jossey-Bass Inc., Publishers

goal-attainment perspective assesses value as a function of how much and how well a program did what it was intended to do. The *cost-benefit* perspective assesses value as the relationship between the consumption of resources and the quantity and quality of benefits received. The most appropriate perspective depends on the stakeholders' or the evaluator's point of view. Often when evaluating recruitment and retention programs, an evaluator will draw on all three of these perspectives (Talmage, 1982).

It is important to remember that because evaluation can be used to justify the allocation of resources (financial, human, technological), it serves a political function. It is precisely this political function that often creates a delicate environment around an evaluation process. Ideally, appropriate evaluation criteria should be established when the program is designed. Too often, however, evaluation is attempted as an afterthought, and evaluators attempt to establish criteria long after the program has been established. As a result, the process becomes ladened with emotion, clouded by uncertainty, and charged with political intrigue. Faced with a situation where evaluation criteria for a program have not been established, it is important to determine the intent and scope of the evaluation before beginning. In this chapter I discuss the intent and scope of evaluation, the role of the evaluator, and the types of evaluation and explore, in some detail, performance indicators that an institution can use to evaluate recruitment and retention programs.

Establishing the Intent and Scope of an Evaluation

The intent of an evaluation may be to reassure politicians or other resource providers, it may be to justify the allocation of resources, or it may be to point out what went wrong with a program or how to make improvements. The first step an evaluator must take in developing an evaluation strategy for recruitment and retention is to determine the intent and the scope of the evaluation to be conducted. The intent of the evaluation has a significant impact on the type of evaluation conducted and enables evaluators to anticipate the major demands for evaluation. Generally, the intent of an evaluation is shaped by one of three conditions: (1) An institutional management philosophy mandates ongoing evaluation to guide program and policy development and resource allocation. (2) Internal or external stakeholders mandate an evaluation. (3) An emergency (or precipitating incident) poses an immediate threat to institutional health. Any or all three of these conditions may exist at any given time in an institution. The most effective institutions in terms of evaluation capability are those where the first condition exists and hence strategies are in place to monitor performance on a regular basis. The intent of ongoing evaluation of recruitment and retention programs is to monitor the performance of people, programs, policies, and procedures in relation to stated goals and objectives.

The scope of an evaluation also must be defined. Evaluation can be narrowly focused or comprehensive. A program can be evaluated to determine its value, efficiency, or effectiveness. Evaluation can be used to determine the performance of people, programs, and systems, to guide decision making, or to determine the impact of strategy, tactics, and operational procedures. The scope of the evaluation must be appropriate to the resources available to conduct the process. A typical evaluation schedule for a recruitment program might include annual performance appraisals of recruitment staff, annual evaluation of recruitment unit performance against stated goals and objectives, annual review of recruitment unit goals and objectives prior to finalization for the following year, annual evaluation of yields by a high school, transfer school, or graduate recruitment program, a biannual survey of parents and guidance and transfer counselors, or biannual analysis of competitors' yields (percentages of accepted students who actually enroll).

Role of the Evaluator

The evaluator must not confuse his or her role with that of the decision maker. The evaluator provides information and perspectives that help the decision maker make the most informed decision. The decision itself may involve factors that were not part of the evaluation. In fact, the decision maker may not follow the most "logical" suggestions of the evaluator. An understanding of the factors that affect decision processes is an important adjunct to understanding evaluation. The most important factor affecting decisions is human nature. Decisions can also be influenced by constituent reactions, organizational culture, local, state, or national environmental conditions, organizational processes or procedures, the influence of institutional leadership, or the natural ambiguity of the decision process (Keller and McCreery, 1990).

The role of the evaluator can be confusing. Evaluators can be left to sort out their own charges, or directives may be vague and subject to interpretation. The primary role of the evaluator is to provide a fair, reasonably balanced assessment that addresses the goals of the evaluation. Within this context the evaluator can and should play a collaborative role. It is important to remember that both faculty and students play a key collaborative role in the evaluation process for both recruitment and retention. Faculty and students must be encouraged to actively participate in the development of recruitment and retention policy, procedures, and strategies.

A fair, logical charge and process should be developed and accepted prior to beginning the evaluation process. Development of the charge for evaluation requires working with the executive officers of the institution (vice-president of academic affairs, vice-president of student affairs, and so on), those being evaluated (admissions, financial aid, school deans, and so on), faculty, and students. In setting forth the charge the evaluator must take care to provide a clear and concise statement on what is being evaluated, a description of the process to be utilized, adequate and appropriate means for input into the process by stakeholders in the program being evaluated, and the opportunity for explanation and rebuttal of findings. Much of the potential success of an evaluation can depend on how well the proper role of the evaluator is established prior to the commencement of the evaluation process.

Types of Evaluation

There is a great deal of literature on the many different types of evaluation methodologies. Evaluations can include descriptive-intuitive undertakings, surveys of internal or external constituents or clients, statistical analyses of performance data, and comparative analyses of performance data from comparable programs.

Evaluations can be classified as formative or summative. Formative evaluations are used to aid the development of a program and include such components as an assessment of student needs and priorities designed to discover unmet student needs; systems assessments designed to determine, for example, if the student record system can support future functions such as voice registration, on-line advising, or integrated student accounts; and process assessments designed to determine, for example, the efficiency and effectiveness of the registration process or the financial aid application and disbursement process. In contrast, summative evaluations assess the overall effectiveness of a program and include such components as program eligibility certifications, financial aid compliance assessments, and program audits. Evaluations can be conducted at predetermined times within a program's life cycle, on a routine schedule such as annually or biannually, or as needed and unannounced.

A Framework for the Evaluation of Recruitment and Retention

In order to establish the appropriate context for evaluating recruitment and retention programs, it is useful to view them within a broader institutional concept of *strategic enrollment management*. This concept is defined as a comprehensive process designed to achieve and maintain the optimum recruitment, retention, and graduation rates of students, where "optimum" is defined within the academic context of the institution (Dolence, 1989a). For some institutions "graduation" (receipt of a degree) may be substituted with "attainment" (achievement of a degree or nondegree objective). Optimum means that the maximum number of students are recruited, retained, and graduated given the academic policies, quality, diversity, resources, and potential of the institution (Dolence, Miyahara, Grajeda, and Rapp, 1988).

The concept of strategic enrollment management is useful because it establishes a linkage between the recruitment and retention programs and the academic program. For purposes of this discussion, recruitment is defined as the active process that an institution undertakes to favorably influence a student's decision to attend the institution. Retention is defined as the maintenance of a student's satisfactory progress toward his or her pedagogical objective until it is attained. Recruitment, then, focuses on pre-enrollment decision processes and retention focuses on postenrollment decision processes (Dolence, Miyahara, Grajeda, and Rapp, 1988).

Many campus administrators mistakenly assume that student matriculation and persistence decisions are primarily a function of administrative activities. They assume that new student enrollments are the product of an effective admissions office, or that high dropout rates within their student populations can be solved by implementing one simple program. The strategic elements of recruitment and retention are primarily academic and not administrative in nature. In fact, the roots of all successful recruitment and retention programs are found in the institutions' academic programs. Strategic academic decisions relate to such tasks as maintaining a balance between academic and professional programs; deciding how many students to enroll; establishing optimum recruitment, retention, and graduation rates; and devising faculty development, rejuvenation, and replacement strategies. These strategic academic decisions form the basis for effective recruitment and retention and should be evaluated along with tactical and operational areas such as admissions, financial aid, and registration (Dolence, 1989a).

Failure to conceptually link recruitment, retention, and academic programs can lead to substantial misconceptions about recruitment and retention problems. For example, a common misconception is that a decline in enrollments is primarily an external phenomenon to which institutions must respond but over which they have no control (Hardy, 1987). Any decline in enrollments is far more likely to be caused by internal failures than by external forces, and the academic program is usually equally culpable with administrative functions.

Effective planning is essential to the maintenance of optimum enrollments in a period of declining applicant populations and should be examined in any evaluation of recruitment and retention programs. More often than not there are serious deficiencies in planning in institutions where enrollments are in decline or student retention is a problem. The use of a formal strategic planning methodology that integrates enrollment management with campus strategies in other areas, such as academic affairs and student life, significantly enhances the overall success of an institution. The strategic planning process should ensure that individual departments play a role in developing and implementing both recruitment and retention strategies. It should also require the evaluation of departmental strategies, policies, and efforts in order to determine their impact on recruitment and retention.

The role of leadership is another key factor in establishing the context for an institution's enrollment management efforts and must be considered when evaluating recruitment and retention programs. Enrollment management efforts should be directed by a clear, concise, written charge, stating in unambiguous terms who is responsible, articulating a commitment to make decisions, and expressing a commitment to implement strategies. There should also be a discernible, integrated campus enrollment management philosophy articulating the desired state of affairs. One such statement indicated that the institution has achieved the optimal numeric enrollment and now seeks to shift the distribution of students to 40 percent graduate, while increasing the average SAT (Scholastic Aptitude Test) scores of entering freshmen by forty points. A statement such as this provides clear direction and priorities for decision making and evaluation.

Participation, coordination, and cooperation among administrative staff are also important elements to examine during the evaluation of recruitment and retention programs. One of the primary reasons for tactical and operational failures is lack of cooperation and coordination between units. A well-developed strategic planning process helps to establish the grounds for cooperation between units. The use of a representative group (perhaps a planning committee) to explore and recommend options for recruitment, admissions, retention, and graduation is an effective way to ensure broad participation. Evaluation processes designed to determine the effectiveness of enrollment management efforts should be closely coordinated with ongoing planning and management schedules. Timing is an important issue and should be evaluated. It is no easy task to align recruitment and retention efforts with academic program evaluation and development processes and with institutional decision and budgeting processes, or to dovetail the evaluation process with strategy review and policy formulation (Hossler, 1984).

Effective management of enrollments requires adequate information support systems. Increasingly these systems are playing a strategic role in enrollment management. Systems such as touch-tone and voice registration, on-line advisement, integrated student accounts, and integrated course scheduling and registration can provide a significant competitive advantage to an institution. Accurate, secure, and available data to facilitate research and evaluation are also absolutely necessary. An assessment of the information systems is integral to any strategy for evaluating recruitment and retention programs.

Human and financial resources are always scarce. There is commonly a rift between senior administrators, who stress that existing resources must be used differently, and managers, supervisors, and staff, who maintain increased resources are required to promote change. The resource allocation and decision-making processes are a legitimate evaluation target. A well-formulated strategic plan helps keep a focus on the task of working within existing resources. Keep in mind that institutions that utilize consensus building, or that link objectives directly to the work plans of managers, supervisors, and staff, indicate a high degree of satisfaction with the resource allocation process. Evaluating the costs and feasibility of ideas too early in the strategy formulation process seriously weakens the process.

Asking Questions

Two particularly important roles for the evaluator are "asking the right questions" and "asking questions right." Asking the right questions is never easy or straightforward. Questions are designed to collect information. Without a succinct idea of what information is needed, the question asking quickly digresses into "what would it be nice to know." This leads to profound confusion as to what is being evaluated, and occasionally to a political interpretation that the evaluation is really a witch-hunt (Sudman and Bradburn, 1982). As Lolli (this volume) points out, a poorly designed evaluation process collects far more data than can be effectively used and increases the cost of evaluation. When trying to make sense of such a myriad of data, the analytic process frequently becomes moribund. It is important to develop a keen sense of what needs to be learned from the evaluation.

Evaluators should refrain from formulating specific evaluation questions until they have detailed the specific dimensions to be evaluated and the information (research questions) needed to proceed. Before deciding on a question, it is important to ask, "How does this question address the specific elements agreed on for evaluation?" A fuzzy answer indicates a bad question. Once the research questions have been determined, evaluators should write them down and refer to them often.

Asking questions right is a highly specialized undertaking fraught with pitfalls. If the evaluator is a beginner or a novice, a little research on the task of asking questions is well worth the time spent. When asking questions, make them as specific as possible. When using multiple choice questions, make sure all reasonable responses are covered. Make sure the time period covered by the question is appropriate to the behavior being addressed. If the subject matter is threatening, open-ended questions are better than multiple choice questions, long questions using familiar words are better than short jargon-laden questions, and the use of data in the question may improve the quality of response. Placement of threatening questions at the end of the questionnaire may also improve the quality of response (Sudman and Bradburn, 1982).

An evaluation matrix is a useful tool in the development of effective research questions. Table 1 outlines a sample evaluation matrix that focuses

Table 1. Sample Evaluation Matrix for Recruitment and Retention

Criteria	Decisions	Information and Data	Process	People and Performance
Leadership	Are decisions made with cognizance of environmental trends, institutional strengths, weaknesses, values, and resources?	Are data collected and analyzed consistent with the decisions faced by the institution?	Is the strategic direction set through a formal planning process?	Are the communication processes of the institution adequate to sustain a strategic focus?
Comprehensiveness	Are individual and unit responsibilities clearly articulated and understood?	Is the quantity of data analyzed sufficient for good judgment and confidence?	Are processes reviewed and revised to eliminate redundancy?	Are the right people involved in the management of enrollments?
Timing	Are decisions made in a timely manner?	Is information made available in a timely manner?	Do processes ensure that tasks are accomplished in the least amount of time?	Does work flow ensure that tasks are accomplished on time?
Systems	Are appropriate technologies available and used effectively and efficiently?	Is the quality of the data sufficient to ensure reasonable accuracy and confidence?	Are data available to and easily manipulable by those who need it?	Are appropriate technologies used effectively and efficiently?
Resources	Are resource decisions made in a way that maximizes the effective and efficient use of resources?	Are adequate information resources and strategies available for management and planning?	Do the processes need to be reengineered, that is, completely redesigned?	Are the numbers of people in line with similar programs at other, comparable institutions?
Strategies	Are decisions made consistent with declared strategies and tactics?	Are data viewed as a strategic asset, and is there a long-term data strategy?	To what degree are strategies and tactics implemented?	To what degree are strategies and tactics effective?

Key performance indicators	Are there clear indicators of success with respect to recruitment and retention, and are they articulated and understood?	Are the indicators measurable and are data available routinely?	Are the indicators of success monitored in an appropriate time frame?	Are the indicators of success tied to units and individuals?
Definitions and classifications	Are there adequate definitions and classifications in place to facilitate communication?	Is there a data dictionary, who is responsible for it?	Is there a process to keep procedures, definitions, and classifications current?	Are organizational definitions and classifications appropriate for the strategies employed?
Participation	Is there adequate participation by constituents in decision making?	Is information shared in an appropriate manner?	Is there a formal consultative/participative process employed?	Do people feel they are part of the strategy of the institution?
Assessments (formative)	Are the results of formative assessments used in decision making?	Is the quantity and quality of information used in formative evaluation adequate?	Is there a strategic assessment schedule?	Is the quality of formative assessments adequate?
Evaluation (summative)	Are the results of summative program evaluation used in decision making?	Are data made available to units and managers on a routine basis for the purposes of monitoring and self-evaluation?	Are the evaluation processes part of policy, conducted on a regular schedule, and distributed appropriately?	Are people and programs evaluated on a regular basis? How are the evaluations used?
Documentation	Are decisions documented and recorded?	Are historical data adequate to facilitate planning and guide decision making?	Is there a formal documentation strategy present?	Are people encouraged to have an institutional perspective or is a parochial/departmental/turf perspective prevalent?

on institutional effectiveness in recruitment and retention across twelve criteria using four specific dimensions. This sample evaluation matrix was in fact used to produce the preliminary evaluation of recruitment and retention activities at one institution. Excerpts from the evaluation follow:

> The enrollment management program suffers from a lack of direction. No formal strategic plan or coordinated, organized process exists for setting forth logical plans for the future. There is an absence of useful program evaluations to guide policy or operational development, and people are evaluated only occasionally. No key performance indicators have been articulated by any of the units. When asked if the members of the enrollment management team should be evaluated against the number of enrollments, they pointed out that appropriate research and information was lacking to guide meaningful recruitment and retention strategies. There was confusion concerning the "alleged retention problem." The enrollment management staff believe that the academic program is out of touch with reality. They allege that new academic policies designed to increase the quality of students attracted to the institution have scared away traditional populations and increased the drop-out rate. There is little or no participation of faculty or academic affairs administrators in the goal-setting, strategy formulation processes of the enrollment management group. There has also been no dialogue concerning the impact of academic policy on recruitment and retention with the enrollment management group.

Evaluating Recruitment

There are many administrators, staff, and evaluators who think that if an institution is not in enrollment decline, then it is not necessary to take the evaluation of recruitment and retention seriously. This conclusion is not true. Recruitment involves many more strategies than those designed to achieve numerical goals of enrolled students. The recruitment program is the primary vehicle for changing an institution's student profile and is therefore a strategic tool of institutional management and should be evaluated as such.

Recruitment and the student enrollment decision processes rest on two primary sets of variables, one related to students and the other to the institution. Student variables include ability, socioeconomic background, input from influential advisers, aspirations and values, geographical considerations, high school characteristics, and expectations about college (Jackson, 1982). Institutional characteristics include price, location, reputation, academic program orientation, sponsorship and control, and physical plant (Chapman, 1981).

The student's decision to enroll is reached through analysis of these variables, based on a perceived alignment or fit between the student's needs and priorities and the institution's programs, services, and characteristics (Hossler, 1984). This alignment between the student's needs and priorities and the institution's programs and services is a focal point of evaluation of the recruitment process. Students make a great many decisions before the final decision of enrollment. Decisions on matters such as which schools to investigate, which schools to submit applications, and which offer of admission to accept are obvious. But decisions about from whom to seek advice, where to look for information, whose advise is most important, and what constitute the most important institutional characteristics are often more subtle and require attention and evaluation. Knowledge about one's students, one's competitors, and the nature and timing of the interchange between them can yield some competitive advantages. Institutions should be active in the process of assessing who is attracted to which institutional characteristics and plan to create or enhance characteristics that strengthen their respective recruitment pictures.

Adequate recruitment structures vary by institution. Generally, targets and strategies should be evident for each level of enrollment within the institution (undergraduate, graduate, professional, continuing education). Further, the institution's markets should be well defined. One of the quickest ways to define geographical markets is to use a formal market classification system such as the Enrollment Planning Service of the College Board (1984). This particular system provides the opportunity for a detailed analysis of core markets and competitive positions relative to other institutions. Definition of market areas by clusters of contiguous zip codes permits the analysis of relevant socioeconomic market information provided by on-campus as well as off-campus sources. A system such as this also enables institutions to focus on and understand particular geographical opportunities, restraints, and targets.

Yield analysis is another important tool used in the evaluation of recruitment programs. Yield is the proportion of students enrolled among those admitted within a targeted group. Yield can be calculated for a variety of groups, such as the high school, community college, or transfer institution that the students attended prior to enrolling, or it can be calculated based on recruitment campaign tactics. It also can be calculated for the zip codes in which the students reside, their scores on the SAT or American College Test (ACT), or their specific disciplines of interest. Yield analysis is a primary tool used in the evaluation of specific strategies and tactics.

A variation on yield is an analysis of the institution last attended (ILA) by the student. ILA is related to yield but facilitates insights into the perceptions and decision patterns of transfer students in key feeder institutions. The data for ILA analysis are collected by tracking key student variables of the institution last attended. These variables might include academic adviser, major course of study, class standing, or even specific faculty. This specificity is required for local and regional recruitment campaigns with a heavy emphasis on faculty relations with the feeder institutions.

Ongoing monitoring of the performance of the recruitment program is essential to good enrollment management and the maintenance of effective recruitment strategies and tactics. To assist in ongoing monitoring, it is helpful to maintain a list of institutional key performance indicators (KPIs) for both recruitment and retention. KPIs are defined as readily available numbers (such as yield, full-time equivalent enrollment, SAT/ACT scores, financial aid participation, and entry-level math test scores) by which the campus can measure success or failure of strategies and tactics as well as progress toward meeting stated goals and objectives.

The central elements of a good evaluation process for recruitment include regular monitoring and reporting of enrollment data; assessment of the data in academic department program review processes; regular evaluation of recruitment campaigns for yield; monitoring of student and parent perceptions, needs, and priorities; and utilization of the evaluations to guide management and planning.

Evaluating Retention

The most important prescription for effective student retention is cooperation and collaboration between the academic and student affairs areas. There are important synergies between the institutional goals of providing a quality education, ensuring successful student development, and fostering high persistence rates among students. Factors affecting the student's decision to continue include grades, program practicality (course of study will lead to a career), individual motivation, assimilation into campus life (for example, club membership, participation in campus events, campus friendships), campus processes (for example, getting the courses one wants, being treated fairly and advised appropriately), professional opportunities (for example, to transfer, work, play sports), and personal situations (for example, marriage, tragedy, pregnancy) (Hossler, 1984). To address this array of factors, the retention program must be an institutionwide priority, supported by quality research, and it must foster a supportive and nurturing environment, focused on the full development of the student, and involve effective academic advising.

While retention has received an extraordinary amount of attention over the past few years, institutions often report disappointment in their ability to significantly alter their respective retention pictures. An important component for those reporting satisfaction with their retention program was the development of a retention classification system. This kind of system permits the classification and tracking of students through an array of retention categories. It provides important data for research and critical information for evaluation of academic and administrative policies, procedures, and programs. The sample retention classification system shown in Exhibit 1 is a modified version of the system developed by Lenning, Beal, and Sauer (1980), which appeared again in Ferguson, Wisner, and Discenza (1986) and in Dolence, Miyahara, Grajeda, and Rapp (1988), and in Dolence (1989a).

The use of a retention classification system facilitates the tasks of tracking students, identifying those who can benefit from early intervention, and evaluating the effect of academic policies and procedures on student continuation rates. These retention KPIs can also be helpful in refining the recruitment program. Once an institution is able to track and monitor students, an evaluation should be conducted to determine the relationship between student retention status and academic program policies. Such an evaluation, conducted every four to five years, provides an important reference for academic program and policy development.

Exhibit 1. Sample Retention Classification System

1. Persisters: currently enrolled students
   A. Satisfactory Degree Progress: currently enrolled students who are making satisfactory academic progress
   B. Unsatisfactory Degree Progress: currently enrolled students who have completed an insufficient number of units
   C. Unsatisfactory Grade Point Average: currently enrolled students who have an insufficient grade point average

2. Graduates: previously enrolled students who have completed a degree objective

3. Attainers: previously enrolled students who have completed a nondegree objective

4. Transfers: previously enrolled students who are attending another university
   A. Planned: previously enrolled students who came with the intent of transferring and eventually did transfer
   B. Unplanned: previously enrolled students who did not come with the intent of transferring but eventually did transfer

5. Stop-Outs: previously enrolled students who are not attending another university and who maintain a continuing student standing

6. Dropouts: previously enrolled students who voluntarily decided not to enroll, are not attending another university, and do not maintain a continuing student standing

7. Dismissals: previously enrolled students who did not enroll due to university action
   A. Disenrollment: previously enrolled students who did not enroll due to university action taken after financial nonpayment
   B. Academic Disqualification: previously enrolled students who did not enroll due to university action after academic disqualification
   C. Administrative Disqualification: previously enrolled students who did not enroll due to university action after administrative disqualification
   D. Disciplinary Disqualification: previously enrolled students who did not enroll due to university action taken as a disciplinary measure

Source: Adapted from Lenning, Beal, and Sauer, 1980.

Conclusion

Effective evaluation of recruitment and retention programs is a critical component of any enrollment management strategy. The most important concept to remember is that evaluation is a strategic tool. It provides staff, managers, and executive officers with the necessary information for informed decision making. Evaluation also serves as a primary policy-making tool and therefore must be grounded within the academic context of the institution. To maximize the effectiveness of the process, evaluation criteria should be established when recruitment and retention strategies are being developed.

Evaluation is also a critical component of strategic planning. As a strategic planning tool it provides vital feedback to guide course corrections and to enhance development of strategies, tactics, goals, and objectives. Because evaluation can be used to guide such critical decisions, it serves a political function, but we must be mindful that political decisions result from bargaining and may not necessarily follow the seemingly logical conclusions of an evaluation.

A number of factors are critical to the success of an evaluation of recruitment and retention programs. First, the evaluation must be guided by a succinct charge stating the intent, scope, and methodology to be used in the process. Second, the evaluation must consider the key academic policies, procedures, and issues relating to recruitment and retention if it is to be helpful in decision making. Third, the research questions and data used must relate directly to the intent and scope of the evaluation to be performed. Fourth, the people involved must be given an opportunity to participate in the evaluation, review findings, and offer responses. Fifth, the information technology support systems must be maintained to provide appropriate, accurate, and available data, as well as tools for analysis. Sixth, the evaluation should be initiated as part of ongoing strategic planning. Seventh, the results of evaluation must be shared and acted on appropriately.

References

Chapman, D. "A Model of Student College Choice." *Journal of Higher Education,* 1981, *64* (5), 490-505.

College Board. *Enrollment Planning Service Program.* New York: College Board, 1984.

Dolence, M. G. "Evaluation Criteria for an Enrollment Management Program." *Planning for Higher Education,* 1989a, *18* (1), 1-14.

Dolence, M. G. "Linking Academic Program Planning and Strategic Enrollment Management." Paper presented at the twenty-fourth annual conference of the Society for College and University Planning, Denver, Colorado, July 24, 1989b.

Dolence, M. G., Miyahara, D., Grajeda, J., and Rapp, C. "Strategic Enrollment Management and Planning." *Planning for Higher Education,* 1988, *16* (3), 13-19.

Ferguson, J. M., Wisner, R. E., and Discenza, R. "Developing a Framework for Student Retention: A Challenge to Traditional Enrollment Approaches." *NASPA Journal,* 1986, *24* (2), 22–29.

Gowen, D. B., and Green, T. F. "Two Philosophers View Education." *Education Evaluation and Policy Analysis,* 1980, *2* (2), 67–70.

Hardy, C. "Turnaround Strategies in Universities." *Planning for Higher Education,* 1987, *16* (1), 9–23.

Hossler, D. *Enrollment Management.* New York: College Board, 1984.

Jackson, G. "Public Efficiency and Private Choice in Higher Education." *Educational Evaluation and Policy Analysis,* 1982, *4* (2), 237–247.

Keller, G., and McCreery, A. "Making Difficult Educational Decisions: Findings from Research and Experience." Paper presented at the annual meeting of the Society for College and University Planning, Atlanta, Georgia, July 31, 1990.

Lenning, O. T., Beal, P. E., and Sauer, K. *Attrition and Retention: Evidence for Action and Research.* Boulder, Colo.: National Center for Higher Education Management Systems, 1980.

Sudman, S., and Bradburn, N. M. *Asking Questions: A Practical Guide to Questionnaire Design.* San Francisco: Jossey-Bass, 1982.

Talmage, H. "Evaluation of Programs." In H. E. Mitzel (ed.), *Encyclopedia of Educational Research.* (5th ed.) New York: Free Press, 1982.

Michael G. Dolence is strategic planning administrator at California State University, Los Angeles. He formerly served as director of research, planning, and policy analysis for the Commission on Independent Colleges and Universities, New York. He has written extensively on strategic enrollment management and information resources management.

Successful systems development requires individuals who are knowledgeable about systems analysis, institutional budgeting processes, and evaluations and have sound interpersonal communication skills.

Creating an Environment in Which Evaluation-Oriented Student Information Systems Can Successfully Compete for Resources

Anthony Lolli

In Chapter One of this volume, Michael G. Dolence discusses a rationale for the evaluation of recruitment and retention programs. The benefits that he describes accrue only to institutions that make the resource commitments necessary to develop student information systems and to conduct evaluation studies. Chapters Three through Seven provide examples of specific activities. They demonstrate what is possible when good planning meets solid execution.

    Sound evaluation of recruitment and retention programs is only possible when information about students is available. The focus of this chapter is on issues that must be addressed in order for evaluation-oriented student information systems to be developed. These issues include the creation of an institutional demand for evaluation, the politics of obtaining resources for system development, and the need for an explicit development plan for institutional administrative computing. The plan must reflect both system functions and benefits as well as costs. I also address how to avoid the problem of evaluation "tail" wagging the processing "dog." The chapter is not a manual for the development of computing systems. Technical skills are necessary, but not sufficient, for creating an environment within which scarce institutional resources can be invested in an evaluation-oriented student information system. This chapter focuses on the issues that, if not addressed, can derail even the most potentially beneficial system before it is implemented. Information systems are essential for successful evaluation. Often the most available and important measures of performance reside within student information systems. For this reason, these systems can be seen as necessary tools for successful evaluations of recruitment and retention activities.

Program Evaluation

Before discussing the major topics of this chapter, it is necessary to briefly describe program evaluation, to contrast program evaluation with personnel evaluation, to contrast program evaluation with research and reporting, and to discuss the implications of program evaluation for systems development.

Program evaluation is the systematic collection of information for the purpose of determining the extent to which program objectives have been met. This definition assumes the existence of explicit, measurable objectives. Such objectives are the products of planning; planning takes time and, in turn, profits from well-executed evaluation (for a description of the role of evaluation in admissions strategic planning, see Lolli, 1988). The absence of such objectives may say something important about an institution's failure to give adequate attention to enrollment management beyond the simplistic contention that more is better (for a more complete discussion of enrollment management, see Litten, 1979; Lay and Endo, 1987; Lay and Maguire, 1982; Hossler, 1984; Lolli and Scannell, 1983).

Program Versus Personnel Evaluation. One of the most important distinctions in our field is between program evaluation and personnel evaluation. It is sometimes a difficult distinction to make and for that reason causes apprehension. As noted above, the intent of program evaluation is to determine the extent to which specific program objectives are met. Failure to meet specific program objectives can be due to several factors, which may not have anything to do with the specific individuals who carry out the program. For example, a goal of doubling applications might be important yet unattainable when the number of high school graduates is in steep decline. Similarly, a system for delivering advisement services via faculty volunteers is unachievable without sufficient volunteers. Poor timing can also cause failure to meet objectives. For example, institutions that provide virtually same-day transfer student services (such as transfer credit evaluation, advisement, and registration) will enroll a significantly higher proportion of admitted transfer applicants than will institutions that spread these services over a longer period of time.

In each of these three examples, programs might fail for reasons unrelated to the quality of personnel involved. Persons who are involved with programs being evaluated may not be familiar with the distinction between program versus personnel evaluation. Such unfamiliarity can lead to suspicion and mistrust, which, in turn, may block a successful evaluation. If one hopes to enlist the necessary cooperation of people involved with programs under review, time should be invested in explaining that the intent and focus of program evaluation is to determine the extent to which program goals have been met.

Evaluation Versus Research Versus Reporting. The finer points of program evaluation, regarding topics such as the distinction between evaluation and research as well as process versus product evaluation, are given extensive treatment in Popham (1975). A review of his text will give the reader a working knowledge of the types of data elements serving each type of evaluation. Briefly, he points out that the goal of research is to draw conclusions, in which generalizability of findings is a highly desirable characteristic. He notes that the central value of research is the discovery of truth. In contrast, evaluation focuses on decision making, and generalizability is less important. The central value of evaluation is the informed decision on whether or not the program under study in fact meets its objectives. In other words, evaluation should be action-oriented. It should enable us to be responsive to changing environments. If environments remain constant, then evaluation could be less frequent. In reality, environments are constantly changing. If campus administrators are to effectively design recruitment and retention programs, then systems that support these activities must provide *early* indications of their effectiveness. It is not sufficient to learn of a program's failures at the conclusion of the program. It is too late to salvage an activity if the evaluation follows the program's conclusion. Reasons for a program's success are equally important. Even though generalizability of findings is not a central focus of evaluation, knowledge of why something works well may be useful in similar situations.

Often, what passes for evaluation is simply a description of the status quo. Such reporting is characterized by its lack of interpretation. It is frequently no more than an extract of raw data that can be summarized descriptively into arithmetic means. Comparisons with previous years or external comparisons with other institutions are not often pursued. It is important to refer to the larger environmental context if evaluations are to be most useful. For example, it is of limited usefulness to know that the number of first-time, full-time, traditional freshmen enrolled as of September 15, 1990, was 975. More useful evaluations are possible with such important reference points as the following: (1) In September 1989, 1,000 first-time, full-time freshmen were enrolled (thus, the 975 represent a decline of 2.5 percent). (2) The demographic change in the primary service area reflected an 8 percent decline in high school graduates (the 975 enrolling freshmen represent an improvement over what might be expected given the market trend). (3) Each of the five major competitors experienced at least a 10 percent decline from last year to this year (in spite of the declining market, greater relative success can be demonstrated vis-à-vis the competition). The placement of institutional performance within a larger context, including trends and comparisons, makes the information more meaningful in regard to the central question of program effectiveness.

Implications of Program Evaluation for System Design

Different types of evaluation serve different purposes (Popham, 1975). Briefly, formative, rather than summative, evaluation is of greater interest for recruitment and retention programs because it permits midcourse corrections of ongoing programs. If information systems are to support formative evaluation, they must not only provide the required information but also make it available in an easily obtainable and timely fashion. If, for example, conversion of African-American applicants from the admitted to the matriculated pool is an important concern for an institution, then certain data must be available. The matriculation decision data for the subgroup must be available on a routine basis. They must be available so that, if need be, resources can be redirected during the late stages of the admissions chronology in order to have a greater positive impact on the group's matriculation decisions. This is a simplistic example, yet it makes a fundamental, albeit obvious, point. Timely data must be easily obtainable if they are to be useful for evaluating programs in progress. Issues such as reporting schedules are germane to system development and must be considered at the time systems are under development if evaluation is to be served by the creation of an administrative computing system.

Each type of evaluation requires different kinds of data and data elements, some of which may already be part of a student information system. Examples of retention-related summative data include final course grades and cumulative grade point averages. Examples of retention-related formative data include midterm grades and participation in extracurricular and cocurricular activities such as student government, newspapers, or intercollegiate athletics.

Some needs may be met by data elements collected on a relatively infrequent basis over a limited period of time, and not collected as part of an existing student information system. For example, changes in a student's intended major may give an early warning of an impending delay of satisfactory progress. Campus administrators and faculty should hope that such student decisions are made with the benefit of advisement on fundamental issues such as additional or different degree requirements. It is not unheard of, however, for students to make decisions in the absence of important information. The subsequent delay of graduation may cause some students to withdraw from school, since, to them, the delay is a sign of failure. If the relationships between changes in student preferences and subsequent decisions to drop or stop out are known, then proactive programs can be developed to help students make the kinds of decisions that lead to success.

Information is potentially both the solution and the problem during the development phase of student information systems. A common mistake during the initial design phases of system development is the attempt to identify every possible student characteristic, academic program datum, and other index that might have some utility, no matter how limited. It is easy to think of all sorts of possible data points that might be nice to know. It is much more difficult for institutional researchers and campus administrators to limit themselves to a list of indices that *must* be known. The combination of a sense of what must be known with a sense of the function of evaluation helps determine the types of data, the treatment of data, the sources of data, and the complexity of subsequent data analyses that are required. Failure to limit data elements to necessary information has the potential of producing system capacity requirements that are too costly to implement. In addition, an overabundance of required data carries an unjustifiable resource requirement of person hours for data entry and file maintenance. A reasonable balance must be struck. It is difficult to justify year-round data collection in support of a semiannual assessment activity. Creation of an advisory committee, representing research, retention, and recruitment interests, can promote such discussions. The advisory committee also yields the additional benefit of fostering stronger working relationships among college constituencies, as later discussed here.

Establishing Institutional Benefits of Evaluation

Contrary to the popular dictum, numbers do not speak for themselves. In order to speak effectively about the need to earmark finite resources for evaluation, evaluators must demonstrate the utility of evaluation by going beyond simple reporting of the status quo. While such reporting is necessary, it is not sufficient. Analysis and interpretation must be available to explain how the status quo came to be. Such interpretation leads to discussions of implications that, in turn, lead to insight regarding specific strategies. Only through such a process can the full value of data be realized. If scarce resources are to be diverted toward expensive computing systems, institutional researchers must demonstrate how such expenditures enhance the effectiveness of recruitment and retention activities through evaluation.

The importance of evaluation varies by institution. In order to obtain an estimate of its importance, the external environment must be understood. An understanding of current and anticipated market forces sets the evaluation agenda for each institution. The task of evaluators would be simple if the status quo on every campus could be maintained indefinitely. In static environments one-time assessments are sufficient. In reality, however, forces operate simultaneously. The first set of factors represents changes within the institution. These include changes in programs and their concomitant changes in demand as expressed by changes in enrollment patterns. The second set of factors relates to activities of competitors designed to obtain more favorable market positions. For example, a competitor's effectiveness in designing new programs could minimize the impact of an institution's well-designed recruitment or retention program. Similarly, an ill-advised academic decision such as changes in graduation requirements could, in the name of academic excellence, drive away marginal but successful students.

An institution that has been shown the potential benefit of analyses such as these is more likely to commit resources to create a student information system capable of supporting evaluation. At the same time, the expectation is created that if the system is developed, a more informed decision-making process will emerge.

System Development

It is beyond the scope of this chapter to provide a detailed discussion of the development of a student information computer system (for a more complete discussion, see Lolli, 1988; Noblitt, 1990; Vesper, 1990). The purpose of this brief section is to describe how institutional researchers can promote the potential benefits of evaluation in order to make it a high priority during the early stages of system development. Early influence on decision making during system development is necessary because the scope of future development activities is often decided early in the process. If evaluation is to become a serious contender for inclusion, it must be placed on the development agenda in the early phase of system definition.

Program evaluation and its complement, strategic planning, can combine to create an impetus for user involvement in system development (for a more expansive discussion of a user-directed model, see Lolli, 1988; Noblitt, 1990). Briefly, the methodology brings together various user constituents in an advisory committee for the purpose of ensuring that each user's information needs, including evaluation, are represented within the development plan. The model also parcels out development responsibilities to each user as a means of achieving user participation.

When researchers are brought together with other professionals, such as admissions practitioners, everyone's understanding of specific, representative office functions is increased. The most important office functions should be represented by system functions. This team-building approach is beneficial because it identifies opportunities for cooperative activities. Of equal importance, it prevents evaluators from being seen by other practitioners as outsiders who are looking over the shoulders of staff who have the primary responsibility for recruitment or retention. Office staff often have a compartmentalized view of responsibilities. It is difficult to appreciate that what occurs in one office has consequences for many other offices. The creation of an advisory committee of users provides a vehicle through which the interrelatedness of offices becomes more apparent. Creation of a user committee also keeps evaluation on the agenda.

The role of evaluation in informed decision making should be emphasized. Evaluators should form partnerships with those responsible for the implementation of recruitment and retention programs. The importance of such partnerships should not be underestimated. Research and evaluative skills are necessary, but not sufficient, if evaluation activities are to be effective. Individuals who are unable to secure the confidence of other professional staff members cannot be effective. Partnerships should also be created with constituencies such as the registrar's office, admissions, student support offices, and faculty. Similarly, the more frequent the opportunities to discuss the importance of evaluation, the greater the likelihood that evaluative functions can be given serious consideration when less-than-ample funds are committed to the development of a computing system.

These partnerships can use their collective voice to stress the importance of system support for evaluation. They can serve to validate the importance of evaluation for the institution. As an additional benefit, partnerships can provide arenas for establishing the high level of trust that must exist among those who participate in evaluation.

Resources and Budget

Partnerships not only increase the likelihood that evaluation data will be useful, they also increase the likelihood of campuswide support for the necessary resources to fund evaluation activities. Many colleges and universities face uncertain futures. College administrators are expected to do more with less. Within this context, every internal constituency competes for funds. Competition exists at several levels, both interdepartmentally and intra-institutionally. The era of declining resources has also increased the need to influence the financial decision-making process as a way to capture necessary funds to support evaluation activities.

Budget Politics. Budgetary processes vary from institution to institution. Regardless of the process, the common necessity is to identify the locus of budget decisions and for those interested in evaluation to become involved. Such involvement in budget decisions may raise difficult turf issues. Those currently in control of computing resources may not welcome the incursion of other campus administrators into what they perceive to be their own realm. By raising questions about widely acknowledged, yet unresolved, budget issues, campus administrators concerned with evaluation of recruitment and retention programs can enter the circle of fiscal decision making as it relates to computing expenditures.

Budgeting and Planning. Does the campus have a plan for administrative computing development? It is not uncommon for an institution to believe that a plan exists. But what passes for a development plan is often inadequate for understanding the process of budget decisions and its implications for evaluation. By pointing out the lack of an explicit development plan for administrative computing that is tied to budgetary realities, campus administrators can lead an institution to confront fundamental questions regarding future choices and directions. Computing represents a growing portion of an institution's expenditures. The planning for such expenditures, however, has often not developed at the same pace. Many institutions, in fact, do not have plans committed to paper. To some extent, this laxity represents the desire of individuals to protect their turf, which is not an acceptable justification for the lack of a formal, explicit, workable plan tied to the budget and shared with appropriate institutional constituents. Individuals who speak for the expenditure of scarce resources have the responsibility to push for the creation of such a plan. The absence of an administrative computing development plan has implications for the ability of individuals to understand how to meet their informational needs in order to evaluate recruitment and retention initiatives. Unless individuals can participate in the development of a plan for future administrative computing, they will not be able to develop attainable goals for evaluation activities.

Establishing the Importance of Evaluation for Management

College and university administrators are routinely called on to make decisions that influence institutional health and vitality. New programs, which require new resources, are proposed and the continuance of existing programs is called into question. In order to make wise decisions, campus managers require evaluative information.

Enrollments as a Means of Including Evaluation in System Design. Given the general fiscal situation and its impact on the availability of funds for computing systems, it may be necessary to clarify the connection between evaluation and revenue. Dollars are becoming scarcer at the same time systems are becoming more expensive. This expense is owing not only to initial purchase costs and necessary maintenance costs but also to the ever-increasing proportion of institutional budgets given over to computer-operating costs. A reasonable planning strategy is to reduce desired system functions to necessary system functions. If a function is not perceived to be essential, it might not be judged worthy of the expenditure. By establishing an evaluation's benefit to the institution's revenue, campus administrators can justify the inclusion of evaluation as a necessary system function. Gone are the days when an institution can overcome high student attrition via increased recruitment. The increased costs of recruitment, as well as the declining number of high school graduates, have eliminated this strategy. As a result a long-term investment in recruitment and retention evaluation capabilities is needed to yield a high return in these programs.

This investment is fundamental to maintenance of the vigor of the institution, and it must be made known to those who control the funds. To some extent, a "chicken and egg" phenomenon exists. Can awareness of the importance of evaluation come before the data are available? Or is the first step to provide data that lead to the awareness? The only suitable resolution of this quandary depends on relatively broad-based discussions within which the benefit of evaluation for revenues can be examined.

Furthermore, participants in these discussions must be aware of institutional funding limitations. Such limitations define the scope of any anticipated systems development. Moreover, since virtually every institution is dependent on tuition revenues, the ability to maintain student enrollments is also central to a positive financial situation. Relationships between the evaluation of recruitment and retention activities and possible funding implications must be developed together.

Expense Versus Return on Investment. Information systems are expensive. Thought must be given to paring down the list of potential evaluation activities. A decrease in size of the list reduces the system support load and therefore reduces not only the initial development cost but also the less obvious yearly costs such as those for data entry and file maintenance. As a starting point, it is important to distinguish what would be nice to know from what is necessary to know. In order to be effective in their requests for resources, evaluators should be able to demonstrate that only the most important evaluation questions have been formulated.

Systems development is expensive enough without the presence of elements that are of limited use for enrollment management. Some pieces of information may be relatively more important than others. Some questions are relatively more important than others. It is important to identify the most cogent pieces of information required. There are no universal guidelines for these deliberations. The constellation of environmental and institutional influences are different for each institution. Recall the distinction between research and evaluation. Questions pertaining to intended outcomes indicate the kind of information to be collected. Information that does not serve evaluation may need to be put aside if funds for systems development are in short supply.

Such consideration has an impact on the kinds of data that should be collected. It also has implications for the expenditure of resources in the course of performing routine activities. For example, if an institution determines that parental level of education is important information in an early warning system for student retention, then it might decide to obtain that data. But the task of recording the information can affect established procedures. The collection of parental educational information may constitute an inappropriate and unwarranted expenditure of data entry time. The fact that the information answers a question that the institution deems important should be considered in the light of the resources required to collect it. Similarly, if the system currently being used does not contain a particular variable, it is important to ask what would be involved in altering the system so as to permit the collection of data on this variable. In the long run, an institution may expend resources that exceed the value of the information collected.

There are less expensive alternatives to administrative computing systems for the collection and storage of data. For example, questionnaires can be distributed to a random sample of students. Existing research can also be used to guide the collection of information. For example, a student's self-reported intent to leave is correlated with actual performance behavior (Bean, 1982). Apparently, students who expect to leave (at the time they enroll) do so at a higher rate than those who report their intention to stay. This knowledge suggests that the educational and career plans of students can be used to help guide the delivery of intervention services. The delivery of necessary services to appropriate students can increase retention.

Such student perceptions, however, need not be reported in a student information system. Data of this type can reside on an off-line file or tape. These research tapes permit a wide array of information on associated variables to be collected and later merged with individual student data. Adoption of merging practices, as opposed to creation of mammoth on-line files, saves expense. The merging of data sets, however, is more complex than working with one on-line file. Merging requires a working knowledge of data management and sufficient disk space for several files. In spite of these inconveniences, the power of today's statistical packages more than makes up for the inconvenience.

Custom-Built Versus Off-the-Shelf Products. Construction of an administrative computing system from scratch is expensive. The purchase of an existing product is also expensive. Often, the investigation of existing products is undertaken with the assumption that off-the-shelf products do not require after-market changes or additions. The expectation is that dollars can be saved if an off-the-shelf product can provide necessary functions without alterations. Too often, the desire to save dollars, at the expense of necessary system functions, leads to disappointment and problems.

Each institution has idiosyncratic processes. It is not possible for an off-the-shelf product to accommodate every possible institution-specific need. For this reason, campus administrators should be prepared to change institutional processes to match product function processes, to supplement the product by adding system functions, to change the product's architecture by altering built-in functions, or to ask users to accommodate system shortcomings. This fourth alternative, unfortunately, is often the default solution. It requires users to support the system, and the institution misses the opportunity to have a system that supports users. As a result, the initially anticipated value of the purchased product is diminished.

There is a way to minimize problems such as this, but it is often overlooked. Necessary discussions often do not take place between people who purchase systems and people who use the systems. Many potential problems resulting from inappropriate purchase choices could be prevented if previous purchasers were consulted regarding their experiences with the product under investigation. Once again, it is not sufficient to speak only with individuals who select and purchase systems. Discussions should also be held with the current users. The purpose of such discussions is to make informed decisions about the pluses and minuses of different products.

Another frequent consequence of the installation of new administrative computing systems is that previously existing functions—often, evaluative reporting capabilities—are lost. These functions, after-market additions to the old system, disappear when a new system, incapable of supporting them, is installed. This results in the loss of previously existing support for administrative practices. If the functions are necessary, an intermediate manual process can be established to regain the capability. As a result, people are once again supporting the system rather than the system supporting the people.

Summary

An environment that values evaluation as a means of effectively using limited resources is a prerequisite for the development of administrative computing systems. An appreciation of the contributions of evaluation to program effectiveness and institutional revenues is required if necessary expenditures are to be committed to create student information systems capable of supporting the evaluation of recruitment and retention programs. This commitment depends on an awareness of, and ability to successfully navigate among, potential pitfalls to funding. Even though technical skills are necessary for effective systems development, the ability to develop a consensus among people with competing interests is more important. Too often campus administrators have treated computing resources as if they were available in an unlimited supply. If this assumption was ever warranted, it is even less warranted now in an era of diminishing resources. Student information systems need to be carefully designed within the constraints of computing hardware, software, and data collection limitations. A collaborative process in the development of student information systems can increase the likelihood that useful information will be available for an array of users who wish to evaluate the effectiveness of recruitment and retention programs.

References

Bean, J. P. "Student Attrition, Interventions, and Confidence: Interaction Effects in a Path Model." *Research in Higher Education,* 1982, *17* (4), 291–320.

Hossler, D. *Enrollment Management: An Integrated Approach.* New York: College Board, 1984.

Lay, R. S., and Endo, J. J. (eds.). *Designing and Using Market Research.* New Directions for Institutional Research, no. 54. San Francisco: Jossey-Bass, 1987.

Lay, R. S., and Maguire, J. "Identifying Distinctive Groups in a College Applicant Pool." *Research in Higher Education,* 1982, *16* (3), 195–207.

Litten, L. "Market Structure and Institutional Position in Geographic Market Segments." *Research in Higher Education,* 1979, 2 (1), 59–83.

Lolli, A. "Strategic Planning: A Crucial Activity for Admissions Success." In *The Admissions Strategist,* no. 12. New York: College Board, 1988.

Lolli, A., and Scannell, J. "Expanding the Focus of Admissions Marketing Utility." *College and University,* 1983, *59* (1), 5–27.

Noblitt, M. T. "Case Study: How Information Systems Support Enrollment Management." In D. Hossler, J. P. Bean, and Associates (eds.), *The Strategic Management of College Enrollments.* San Francisco: Jossey-Bass, 1990.

Popham, W. J. *Educational Evaluation.* Englewood Cliffs, N.J.: Prentice-Hall, 1975.

Vesper, N. "Understanding and Designing Student Information Systems." In D. Hossler, J. P. Bean, and Associates (eds.), *The Strategic Management of College Enrollments.* San Francisco: Jossey-Bass, 1990.

Anthony Lolli is vice-president for enrollment management and student services at William Paterson College, Wayne, New Jersey.

One institution's experiences in exploring the impact of institutional contacts provide insights into the development, evolution, and changes in admissions procedures.

Evaluating the Impact of Institutional Contacts

Marian F. Pagano, Dawn Geronimo Terkla

Over the past thirty years, a body of literature has emerged that attempts to explain why certain individuals attend college and others do not. In some instances this college choice literature has been further refined to the point of describing why individuals choose to matriculate at a particular type of institution. In addition to this research, there are institution-specific studies that attempt to explain why certain individuals choose to attend a specific institution. One commonality in this research is the finding that institutional characteristics and college environments are among the critical factors in determining the college choice decision. Institutional contacts, both formal and informal, reflect and communicate the personality of the institution. As a result they help shape the image prospective students and their parents have regarding the institutional environment. Thus, it is imperative to understand the impact of these contacts. (For purposes of this chapter, institutional contacts refer to the multiplicity of interactions that prospective students or their parents have with the institution. These interactions may include, but are not limited to, such things as campus tours, alumni interviews, literature about the institution, formal contacts with university personnel, and informal interactions with current students.)

Historical Background

Evaluation of the impact of institutional contacts has been an implicit, and at times explicit, objective of the admissions research agenda at Tufts University since the early 1980s. Although admissions-related research has been conducted at the institution for several decades, formal survey research of

NEW DIRECTIONS FOR INSTITUTIONAL RESEARCH, no. 70, Summer 1991 © Jossey-Bass Inc., Publishers

specific constituencies began in 1981. (The current piece concentrates on survey research. There are a variety of other techniques, especially qualitative ones such as focus groups, which others may want to pursue to further understand the impact of their institutional contacts.)

In the initial stage of the research an annual survey was designed and administered to the accepted applicant population, those individuals who applied and were offered admission to the institution. The primary objective of these early surveys was to identify the students' institutional choice sets and those factors that most influenced their final, college choice decisions. In those early surveys, there was at least one question that attempted to garner evaluative information regarding the impact of institutional contacts. Typically, accepted applicants were asked to indicate the magnitude (from strongly positive effect to strongly negative effect) that various factors, such as a personal interview on campus or contact with admissions representatives at a local high school, had on their decisions to enroll at a particular college or university.

As the competition for students has become keener and as resources have become scarcer, there has been a growing interest in evaluating the impact of institutional contacts. This interest is reflected in an expansion of questions in the annual survey. Not only have more comprehensive questions been posed to the accepted applicant population but the study of additional populations affected by the interactions has been initiated. Specifically, Tufts has evaluated the impact of institutional contacts on individuals who made inquiries about the institution but did not submit an application, and on the parents of matriculating students.

Question Development and Evolution

The most important step in evaluating institutional contacts is deciding the appropriate questions to ask. Questions should cover all potential contacts that students have with the institution. An institutional contact can take on many forms, some of which are directly controlled by the institution, such as mailed materials and guided tours. Others are not, such as random encounters with alumni by prospective students and informal campus visits. All of these contacts have an impact on the prospective student's impression of the university.

Prime targets for evaluation are the special programs or events an institution creates and finances in order to promulgate the unique qualities of the institution. Commonly used programs include campus tours, admissions-sponsored overnight visits, weekends or weeks for all applicants, accepted students, or special populations (such as engineers or minority students), campus videotapes, and local area receptions. The goal of the evaluation is to discover which programs or events are having a positive influence on students' impressions of the institution and which are having a negative influence.

When evaluating a program, it is helpful to break the program down into its components. For example, formal campus tours have a great influence on students' impressions of the institution. Information concerning the length of the tour, content, size, and knowledge and friendliness of the guide can be used to play to the strength of this influential event. The evaluation can be used to fine-tune these components to the point where the overall tour can be monitored with fewer evaluation questions.

Not all potential contacts are readily apparent to the institutional researcher or admissions officer. It is safe to assume that the range of contacts will vary from institution to institution. Even at a single institution, contacts may vary from one year to the next. One of the goals in developing a survey instrument is to make the instrument as inclusive as possible. An effective strategy for inclusiveness is to utilize open-ended questions during the first stages of the research, whether these constitute a pilot test or the first year of survey administration. By utilizing an open-ended format, prospective students can provide valuable information on a variety of contacts. Even with only one open-ended question, the researcher can collect a reasonably accurate list of the sources. For example, institutions that attempt to collect data on the influence of institutional contacts are better served by the first question than by the second:

1. Please list below the five sources that provided you with the most helpful information concerning your decision to attend (not to attend) University X.

2. Please indicate to what degree the following sources influenced your decision about University X:
   campus tour
   interview
   catalog
   video
   local reception

By prefabricating a list, one runs the risk of losing valuable information because it is impossible to be aware of all influential contacts. However, once the information is obtained from administering the first question, it would be perfectly reasonable to construct a question similar to the second and use it for future research purposes. Therefore, the evolution and refinement of questions, accomplished over a period of several years, are key assets in collecting data on institutional contacts.

Admissions researchers should always be cognizant of changes in institutional policies that might affect institutional contacts. For example, an institution recently moved into the National Collegiate Athletic Association (NCAA) Division I, thereby allowing it to expand its athletic scholarship program. This was a highly publicized change throughout the school's usual market area and beyond. The institutional researchers believed that this change would positively influence their image and responded by including questions in their survey that probed the attitudes of accepted applicants toward this change. The information garnered from the survey determined the extent to which their new NCAA classification was highlighted in later university publications.

It is important to understand both the formal and informal contacts that individuals have with an institution. Researchers have a tendency to fall into the trap of only evaluating formal contacts because they feel that these are the only kind of manipulable variables. As a result, researchers and admissions officers often view brochures, visits, and telephone calls as key contacts. But there is contrary evidence. For instance, many schools have discovered that informal contacts with current students, especially those from their respective hometowns or local high schools, are especially influential on prospective students' impressions of the institutions, although the influence is not readily apparent. One college, upon discovering this power of informal contacts, mounted a large and loud internal public relations effort. Professionally created newsletters detailing the achievements of current students and recent graduates were circulated to current students, keeping them apprised of the positive experiences of their peers. Over time it was found that this information had trickled down to their friends and former classmates who were considering the school.

In addition to creating an array of questions that cover a diverse range of institutional contacts, questions should gather information about the quantity, frequency, and timeliness of the contacts (such as visits to the campus), as well as the quality of the contacts (such as meetings with faculty or coaches). Exhibit 1 presents sample questions designed to elicit such information.

Not only is it important to know whether prospective applicants visit one's institution; it is important to know when they visited. Strategies can be developed to provide different types of information for individuals at various stages. The type of contact and information required by a student in his or her junior year in high school is very different than that required by a graduating senior who has already been accepted for admission at the institution.

Understanding the types of influence that various contacts have on individuals' decision of whether or not to accept an offer of admission provides valuable information to an institution. For instance, contacts identified as having a negative influence can be examined in greater detail and modifications can be made to at least neutralize, if not eliminate, such sources of influence.

In addition to using discrete, traditional survey questions, we urge and support the use of at least one explorative open-ended question on a survey. We have used questions such as "Why do you think you were accepted to

Exhibit 1. Sample Survey Questions on Quantity and Quality of Institutional Contacts

1. Did you visit University X?

___ Yes
___ No

2. Did you visit the school you would have attended?

___ Yes
___ No

3. In the left-hand column please indicate whether you visited University X during each of the specified time periods. In the right-hand column please indicate whether you visited the school you would have attended during any of these time periods.

Yes	No		Yes	No
___	___	a. Prior to junior year?	___	___
___	___	b. During your junior year?	___	___
___	___	c. Summer before senior year?	___	___
___	___	d. Senior year—before applying?	___	___
___	___	e. Senior year—after applying, but before acceptance?	___	___
___	___	f. After acceptance?	___	___

4. For each of the events listed below, please indicate the influence it had on your decision about accepting University X's offer of admission.

very influential   1   2   3   4   5   not influential

a. Meeting with admissions representative at your high school
b. Tour of campus by admissions guide
c. Informal tour of campus
d. Visit to a class(es)
e. Meeting students on campus (exclude tour guides and those known previously)
f. Group information session on campus
g. Contact with faculty or coaches
h. Mail or telephone contact with University X students
i. Overnight stay on campus (arranged informally)
j. Fall meeting in local area
k. Engineering Week or other engineering event
l. Seeing video about University X
m. Alumni interview
n. Informal alumni contact
o. Contact by mail from admissions
p. Contact by telephone with admissions
q. April overnight program for accepted students
r. April program on campus for accepted students
s. April reception in local area
t. Information about University X in the local or national news
u. Information about [city] in the local or national news

Tufts?", "What could we have done to have made the college selection process easier for you and your son/daughter?", "What is your definition of academic reputation?", and "What else would help us understand why you chose (did not choose) Tufts?"

We compile these comments and sort them by their content. They give a qualitative view of the important concepts expressed about the college choice decision. We are often surprised by the frequency with which contacts with other high school students are cited and contacts with Tufts admissions representatives are not cited in this section.

Targeted Populations

Evaluative information about university contacts can be gained at all levels in the admissions funnel. The variety, quality, and quantity of institutional contacts differ across target populations and across individuals as defined by their respective relationships with the institutions. Moreover, there are drawbacks and benefits inherent to the process of querying individuals at various stages in the admissions process.

One population targeted for inquiry is defined as those students who request information from or about the institution but never submit an application for admission. This is the largest group in the admissions funnel with which institutions will have some contact, and at some institutions the rate of contact can be as high as five or more inquiries per prospective applicant. For a variety of reasons, it is difficult to gather information from this group. If an individual makes a written request for information, he or she may or may not include background information. For this group, the only information available may be local mailing addresses. If an individual makes a telephone request for information, the institution may be able to obtain additional background data by developing a prescreening mechanism. But regardless of the amount of information available, when surveying this population, it is important to remember that the individuals discontinue their associations with the institution early on in the admissions process.

When surveying the inquiry pool in general, several issues are important. The survey should be short and convenient. A self-mailing format or postcard is probably best. Space is limited, so it must be used efficiently in order to assess which institutional contacts were made and what impressions resulted from the contacts. Response rates will be low, so it is important to oversample the population in order to ensure that respondents are representative.

One might want to consider conducting telephone interviews with an inquiry population. It is quite likely that a phone survey will improve response rates. However, before embarking on this method of data collection, one should be cognizant of the additional resources that will be needed. Often, the telephone numbers of prospective applicants are not readily available. In order to obtain these numbers, an institution might want to consider contracting with an outside service that specializes in locating telephone numbers. In addition, one should anticipate the need for telephone interviewers who are able to conduct the interviews during evenings and weekends. A bank of telephones and a computer or terminal for each interviewer are important resources to facilitate immediate data entry. If telephone surveying is not a regular function of the admissions office, the cost of collecting the information over the telephone may be prohibitive. But if this method still remains the preferred alternative, one might want to consider contracting with an outside organization that specializes in this type of data collection.

Many institutions send out accepted-applicant surveys. Accepted applicants constitute an intriguing group because it is a mix of those who had a very favorable impression of an institution and chose to matriculate there as well as those who were either unimpressed with the institution or more impressed with another institution and chose to go elsewhere. This contrast sets up an ideal opportunity to see which, if any, institutional contacts significantly differentiate the two groups.

Our research has shown that among all of the individuals who potentially influence a student's college selection, parents have the strongest influence, particularly mothers. Consequently, we have studied the parents of matriculating students. Parents frequently participate in many aspects of the college selection process with their offspring. They take great interest (perhaps even more than the student) in reading college brochures, and they often travel with their children on college visits. In many cases, the students and the parents have an equivalent amount of contact with the institution. Indeed, parents can have more contact with the institution than have the students, especially with respect to the financial aid office and questions surrounding financial assistance—a critical variable in college selection. Parents pay the bills and thus seem to be geared toward a consumer relationship with the college or university. Consumer relationships demand courtesy, service, and a quality educational experience—factors that parents evaluate with respect to institutional contacts.

Analysis and Results of Admissions-Related Research at Tufts

Given the unique nature of each higher education institution, admissions researchers should not assume that the findings for one institution will automatically be germane for another. With this cautionary note, we share here some of the general findings of the admissions-related research that has been conducted at Tufts University over the past ten years.

Inquiries. It is important to conduct evaluation research at every stage of the collegewide process. Admissions marketing is expensive; one cost-effective method of increasing enrollments is to increase the yield between the inquiry stage and the application stage. The primary objective of our research at this stage has been to determine why students who initially showed some interest in the institution eventually chose not to submit an application. Students were asked to indicate their degree of satisfaction with twelve institutional contacts (see Table 1). These items were part of a brief survey that also asked students why they did not apply to Tufts, why they did apply to their first-choice school, why they did not visit Tufts, and where they did apply, as well as requested basic demographic information and entrance test scores. A low response rate was expected, and in fact a response rate of only 10 percent was realized. However, since this was anticipated, a large quantity of surveys (over five thousand) was mailed. We did not know the characteristics of the entire population but made the assumption that the respondents were reasonably representative of the entire population.

As expected, most students did not have a lot of institutional contact at such an early stage in the college selection process. Most of the respondents indicated that the majority of contacts were "not applicable." In general, students were most frequently able to evaluate only the content and timeliness of admissions-related mail and information about the institution in the local and national news. This limited range of experiences is not very startling given that these are the types of contacts most inquiries would elicit.

Beyond these initial contacts we found that approximately 25 percent of the inquiry population had additional contacts of a more personal nature, such as telephone calls to the admissions office, visits to the campus, local college night programs, a formal tour of campus, and the admissions office orientation meeting. Less than 25 percent of the respon-

Table 1. Tufts University Survey Questions on Institutional Contacts and Scale of Satisfaction

Types of Contacts	Scale of Satisfaction
1. Telephone calls to Tufts admissions office	1. Strongly positive
2. Telephone calls from Tufts students	2. Positive
3. Information in admissions-related mail	3. Neutral
4. Visits to Tufts campus	4. Negative
5. Timeliness of admissions-related mail	5. Strongly negative
6. Student/parent meeting in local area	6. Didn't do
7. Information on Tufts in local or national news	
8. Video about Tufts	
9. Contact with Tufts faculty or coaches	
10. Local college night	
11. Formal tour of Tufts	
12. Admissions office orientation meeting	

dents indicated that they had the most personal variety of contacts with the institution, such as telephone calls from current students, student/parent meeting in the local area, and contact with a faculty member or coach.

The more-personal institutional contacts were more likely to be seen as having a positive influence on the student's impression of the institution than were the general, less-personal, large-group contacts. This finding suggests an institution could increase its ability to make a positive impression by increasing the degree of personal treatment focused on inquirers. The problem is that much of the more-personal contact must be initiated by the prospective student. It is simply too expensive and time consuming for the institution to initiate these personal contacts at this early stage of prospective student interest.

Inquiring students seldom attributed their decisions not to apply to institutional contacts. However, there were some contacts, including the timeliness of mailings and campus visits, that received lower than anticipated ratings.

Accepted Applicants. Our data pool for applicants is extensive, encompassing nearly ten years of data on ten entering classes. The method for gathering these data has remained fairly constant: a survey mailed to students shortly after their decisions regarding matriculation have been received by the university. We have been fortunate to have had very high response rates from both the matriculant and nonmatriculant populations (approximately 90 percent and 70 percent, respectively). We believe the key issue here is the timing of the mailing of the surveys. Many, many institutions now send surveys to accepted applicants. The institutions that enjoy the highest response rates are those that mail their surveys soon after receiving word on a student's decision. In informal interviews with incoming freshmen we have learned that they are pleased to fill out the first few surveys they receive as the excitement of having made their college choice and anticipation of attending school motivate their need to communicate. This enthusiasm wears thin as the fourth, fifth, and sixth surveys arrive. It is also our experience that students who have very strong feelings about the institution—either particularly pleased or especially disappointed—are likely to return a survey regardless of the timing.

At Tufts, matriculants receive a slightly different instrument than that sent to nonmatriculants. Both groups of accepted applicants are asked to evaluate the institutional contacts that they have had with the university. These evaluations allow us to make comparisons between those who were favorably impressed with the university at some level and those who felt that another institution better fit their needs. From the university's perspective, all were qualified and had the ability to flourish at Tufts. So for us the key analytical question is, What role did institutional contacts play in separating these two groups? Our surveys over the past ten years have been designed to help us answer that question.

Foremost, we use item 4 in Exhibit 1 to analyze institutional contact. In that particular question we list the events that in our experience most frequently influence impressions. Matriculants and nonmatriculants are asked to indicate how influential each event was on the decision to accept or reject the university's offer of admission. Participation rates of matriculants tend to be higher than those of nonmatriculants. Overall, we have found that nonmatriculants are more likely than matriculants to indicate that an event was either negative or strongly negative.

An interesting phenomenon seems to occur here. As participation increases, the proportion of those who express a negative or strongly negative impression increases. So as institutions have prospective students visit classes or meet students and faculty, each institution runs the risk of a very influential event being perceived as a negative experience. This is not to say that these more intimate events are routinely viewed as negative but rather that the institution puts itself in a precarious situation. This possibility of a negative experience might be especially high for the many prospective students who are unfamiliar with university culture. Their expectations of what a college classroom or professor *should* look like might collide with reality. This mismatch could result in a negative experience that the student attributes to a particular institution, when in reality the student is simply getting his or her first taste of university culture as, for example, manifested in the fashion eccentricities of a physics professor.

Another question that we have used for years in an attempt to ascertain prospective students' perceptions about the university is as follows:

Which statement most accurately describes the attitude of Tufts toward you?

_____ 1. Strong interest in me as a human being

_____ 2. Interested in me for my capabilities

_____ 3. Obliging, but without genuine interest

_____ 4. Just another statistic

In addition to giving us a broad view of how we are perceived by our prospective students, this question differentiates the matriculants from the nonmatriculants. We have found through the years that nonmatriculants are much more likely than matriculants to indicate that the perceived attitude was "just another statistic."

In 1989 we used a new question on both our matriculant and nonmatriculant surveys. It read as follows:

Of the information you received from ALL colleges and universities, which did you find most useful?

_____ 1. Student newspapers

_____ 2. Newsletters

_____ 3. Catalogs

<u>   </u> 4. Letters from admissions officers
<u>   </u> 5. Letters from faculty
<u>   </u> 6. Letters from students
<u>   </u> 7. Phone calls from alumni
<u>   </u> 8. Phone calls from current students
<u>   </u> 9. Phone calls from admissions officers
<u>   </u> 10. Other <u>   </u>

Results from this question have shown that nearly half of both the matriculant and nonmatriculant populations found the catalog to be the most useful source of information. This finding is a little discouraging for those admissions officers who spend hours talking on the phone or conducting local area meetings. But it does emphasize what most of us already know: Mailed information is one of the most important institutional contacts. It is permanent and a reference that interested students will read in great detail. It is the only contact many students will have with the institution. Additional sources of information most commonly cited by accepted applicants included telephone calls from students and student newspapers.

Parents. In a study conducted several years ago, we explored parents' impressions of the university using a six-page survey instrument. Institutional contacts were evaluated for their degree of influence on the son or daughter's college choice, as well as how satisfied the parents were with the contacts as part of the admissions process. The institutional contacts about which we queried were students from Tufts, alumni of Tufts (other than interviewer), alumni interviewer, and admissions officer from Tufts. Approximately 65 percent of the parents reported that each of these contacts had a positive or strongly positive influence on their son or daughter's college choice. It is interesting to note that the alumni interviewer received a strongly positive rating.

Parents were overwhelmingly satisfied with most aspects of the admissions process. Over 50 percent were very satisfied with the quality of the information mailed. They seemed to be least satisfied with the institutional contacts that require direct access to admissions personnel. However, this dissatisfaction was minimal, with only 5 percent indicating some degree of dissatisfaction with the availability of admissions officers. An even smaller proportion of parents expressed dissatisfaction with telephone contacts (although we do not know which particular aspects), alumni interviews, and on-campus interviews (perhaps the lack thereof).

In addition to asking how satisfied they were about various aspects of the admissions process, we asked specific questions about their contacts with the financial aid office. Here, the range of responses was more evenly distributed, filling in the dissatisfaction side of the scale. We presume that at least part of the increase in dissatisfaction with the service is due to dissatisfaction with the size of the financial aid award. We do not mean to minimize the tedious and confusing effects the financial aid application process can have on parents. While students are wooed and may see only the high points and glamour of the institution, parents are faced with the harsh reality of financing an undergraduate education. This is reflected in the comparatively high percentage of parents who expressed dissatisfaction with many aspects of the financial aid office. Approximately 15 percent of the parents indicated some level of dissatisfaction with the overall financial aid process. An examination of the various aspects of the aid process revealed that the lowest levels of dissatisfaction were with the content of the mailings and with the Tufts University financial aid application form. Parents more frequently expressed dissatisfaction with both the availability of professional staff and the telephone contacts with financial aid officers. Their comments later in the survey expressed frustration that they could rarely get someone to listen to and sympathize with their specific situations. They described the process as driven solely by numbers and as impersonal. Some expressed dissatisfaction with the notification process and level of explanation provided.

Implications and Resulting Changes in Procedures

Many impressions that individuals, including institutional researchers, have about an institution are based on anecdotal information. By conducting the type of research described here, not only does one discover some new and potentially interesting information about the institution but also the experience affords the opportunity to confirm hunches or to dispel myths.

This type of research provides an excellent vehicle to monitor how changes in policies and practices are affecting the institution's various constituencies. For example, at Tufts, results from the inquiry survey verified the importance of changes that had been implemented as a result of information from the accepted-applicant survey in previous years. Most notable among these changes are the elimination of on-campus admissions interviews, replaced by interviews with local area alumni, and new policies for routing incoming telephone calls, including increased training for admissions operators.

The inquiry survey showed that only a very small proportion of students did not visit campus because of the unavailability of on-campus interviews. In addition, an accepted-applicant survey conducted after the elimination of the on-campus interviews showed a quite favorable review of the alumni interview. In the latter survey, many students also cited their alumni interviewer as their single best source for information about Tufts.

Finally, it is important to emphasize the need to disseminate admissions-related research findings to key members of the university community. The information gathered has implications for practice within the admissions office, for the creation and modification of publications, as well as for the policies and practices of other members of the university community who have contact with prospective students and their parents. An ongoing admissions research effort enables both the admissions and financial aid offices to further improve their interactions with prospective students and parents. At Tufts, we believe this has increased the effectiveness of our recruitment efforts.

Marian F. Pagano is researcher analyst in the Office of Institutional Research, Tufts University, Medford, Massachusetts.

Dawn Geronimo Terkla is the director of institutional research and planning at Tufts University.

The strategic use of financial aid to advance institutional enrollment objectives is increasing, but more attention needs to be given to assessment of its effectiveness.

Evaluating the Impact of Financial Aid on Student Recruitment and Retention

Lee Wilcox

The critical importance of financial aid as a factor in college enrollments is obvious to even the most casual observer of higher education. The College Board (1990) estimates that nearly $28 billion of financial aid was provided to students in postsecondary education in 1989–1990. Porter and Barberini (1989) note that one-half of all college students receive some form of financial aid.

Over the last decade, the problem of financing college enrollment has become more visible. The national press has been replete with stories about tuition increases that have outpaced inflation. Federal officials such as former budget director David Stockman and former education secretary William Bennett have been highly critical of college practices in setting tuition and other educational costs. Annual efforts by the executive branch to reduce federal financial aid programs have been mostly offset by congressional action. Even so, total federal aid to postsecondary students was 3 percent less in 1989–1990 than what it was in 1980–1981, as measured in constant 1989 dollars (College Board, 1990, p. 7).

The relationship between college costs, family income, and available financial aid shows clearly why financial aid has been getting so much attention. Using constant 1989 dollars, available financial aid increased 10 percent and disposable personal income increased 18 percent between 1980 and 1990. Unfortunately, college costs increased even faster: 18 percent at public two-year colleges, 40 percent at public four-year colleges, 40 percent at public universities, 52 percent at private four-year colleges and universities, and 60 percent at private universities (College Board, 1990, p. 11).

NEW DIRECTIONS FOR INSTITUTIONAL RESEARCH, no. 70, Summer 1991 © Jossey-Bass Inc., Publishers

For many institutions, especially private ones, student aid is a major institutional expense as well as a major revenue source. For example, at Rensselaer Polytechnic Institute in Troy, New York, institutionally funded scholarships represent approximately 26 percent of undergraduate tuition income. Financial aid from outside sources accounts for about 31 percent of tuition income, and family support for the remaining 43 percent. Given these expense and revenue figures, institutional self-interest demands careful study of the impact of student aid on enrollment.

Purposes of Financial Aid

From a societal standpoint, the purposes of financial aid are to provide needy students with access to higher education, reasonable choices among alternative institutions, and financial ability to persist until graduation or achievement of some goal prior to graduation (Huff, 1989). From an institutional standpoint, the purposes of financial aid are somewhat parallel: to help students afford to choose among institutions and, upon making their choices, help them afford to persist to graduation or achievement of some prior goal. In effect the overriding goal is to allow students with financial need to make enrollment choices on the same bases as students without financial need.

During the past decade, demographic and economic trends have had a negative impact on the enrollments at an increasing number of institutions. As a result, financial aid has come to be viewed as more than an equalizer for students with financial need. Financial aid is now also widely recognized for its strategic value in attracting the number, quality, and mix of students desired by an institution. By targeting institutionally controlled aid to students who are most attractive to the institution, the probability of their initial and continued enrollment can be enhanced. Even where aid is insufficient to meet the demonstrated need of all the students, strategic allocation of available aid can be useful in meeting institutional goals.

Methodological Issues

Evaluation of the impact of financial aid on recruitment and retention of undergraduate students involves complex methodological issues. As is so often the case in higher education research, the use of true control groups is seldom appropriate. Principles of equity override statistical considerations in deciding how to allocate financial aid to equally worthy students. The choice of withholding scholarships from one group of deserving students while awarding the same scholarships to an equally deserving group raises obvious ethical problems.

Perhaps even more problematic in the evaluation of financial aid impact is the issue of multiple variables. Both the college choice literature

(Hossler, 1984) and the retention literature (Tinto, 1987) have identified many individual and institutional characteristics, as well as individual-institutional interactions, that are involved in students' enrollment choices. Among the important variables in college choice besides cost and financial aid, Hossler (1984) mentions personal characteristics such as ability, parents' occupations and education, advice of significant others, educational and vocational goals, demographic identity, and geographical locale and institutional characteristics such as academic orientation, location, student life atmosphere, and recruitment practices. Similarly, Tinto's (1987) retention model identifies family background, skills and abilities, prior schooling, student intentions and goals, academic performance, extracurricular activities, faculty and peer interactions, and academic and social integration as important factors in students' decisions to continue or drop out of college. The task of isolating the effects of financial aid on either the decision to enroll at a particular college or to stay enrolled at that college is extremely difficult given the complexity of the variables involved.

Perspectives from the Literature

Institutional studies of the impact of financial aid should be guided by existing research. A review of the research can assist institution-based evaluators to develop evaluation questions and to select appropriate methods of analysis.

Impact on Recruitment. No-need scholarships constitute perhaps the most clear-cut use of financial aid in recruiting new students. These scholarships also have been the fastest growing type of aid in institutional awards. Chapman and Jackson (1987) observed that studies in the late 1970s found that 55–65 percent of four-year colleges offered no-need awards, whereas a College Board/National Association of Student Financial Aid Administrators study in 1984 found that 85–90 percent of four-year colleges offered these awards. And although many aid officers stated that the purpose of these awards was to recognize outstanding achievement, none of the awards was portable to another institution.

A comprehensive multi-institutional study of the impact of no-need scholarships on college choice was conducted by Chapman and Jackson (1987). They surveyed a national probability sample of nearly twelve hundred high-ability high school seniors who were admitted to at least two colleges in 1984. Nearly two-thirds of the students received at least one financial aid offer, and about one-half reported receiving aid based on academic ability. Over two hundred aid offers were received by students who did not even apply for aid.

The authors used a statistical model to assess the determinants of college choice. They found that perceived academic quality was the principal factor determining student preference prior to admissions decisions, that this preference was the major factor in college choice following admissions decisions, and that no-need scholarships had a smaller but significant effect on college choice. Perceived chance of scholarship renewal was also significant, while nongrant forms of financial aid (for example, loans, college-work study) were not.

Chapman and Jackson's model permitted them to estimate the amount of no-need scholarship that would be required to move a second-choice school to first-choice status ($4,700 in 1984 dollars). It also estimated the change in probability of choosing a particular college for each $1,000 of no-need scholarship, as well as the cost of such a strategy at various scholarship levels.

The cost of offering no-need scholarships as an enrollment incentive is complicated by the fact that colleges cannot tell ahead of time who would enroll without the incentive. Thus, the cost of such awards is the sum of the awards to those who would have enrolled without the award plus the awards to those extra students attracted by the award. These costs are offset by the tuition revenues of the extra students.

The practice of awarding no-need scholarships as well as various need-based forms of aid was studied in forty-one Illinois colleges by Anderson, Ellickson, Nuetzel, and White (1985). Most of these colleges (83 percent) and virtually all of the four-year colleges in the group (96 percent) offered no-need scholarships. In addition, many of the institutions reported the packaging of need-based aid to favor specially targeted groups such as high academic ability (59 percent), special talents (42 percent), international (33 percent), preferred curricular (30 percent), disadvantaged (25 percent), and low or no financial need (23 percent).

Zelenak and Cockriel (1986) reviewed several studies on the effectiveness of no-need scholarships in recruitment. They concluded that no-need scholarships are probably not cost-effective at prestigious private colleges but probably would be at moderately priced public institutions of high quality. They observed that institutions using merit-based awards should be aware that such practices may not be consistent with other institutional goals such as maximizing revenue or attracting disadvantaged students.

The effectiveness of no-need scholarships in the recruitment of freshmen at Southwest Missouri State University (SMSU) was studied by Iba, Simpson, and Stockburger (1988). SMSU offers regents scholarships, which cover about 20 percent of the annual institutional cost, to high-ranking seniors without application. Groups of prospects, admitted students, enrolled students, and no-shows were surveyed on the importance of these scholarships to their application or matriculation decisions.

Several findings in this study are noteworthy. Although the offer of an academic scholarship was rated highly by all four groups when asked to name factors in their choice process, most of the students acknowledged that they would have enrolled or applied without a scholarship. Also, the importance of the scholarship in student choice varied by location (lower impact on local students) and by ability (lower impact on high ability). Finally, in comparing hypothetical scholarship offers, an increase in the award from 20 percent to 30 percent had little impact, whereas an increase to 50 percent of institutional cost showed a significant jump in degree of influence.

Impact on Retention. The effect of financial aid on student persistence has been studied more extensively than has its effect on student recruitment. Murdock (1990) found forty-nine studies in the 1952–1986 period that empirically investigated the relationship between financial aid and persistence. She performed a metanalysis on these studies by computing a common index of effect size (effect size is the treatment-group mean minus the control-group mean divided by the control-group standard deviation) and averaging effect sizes for all studies using similar treatment and control groups. Over seventy thousand students were involved in these studies.

The basic research question—Does financial aid improve student retention?—was answered affirmatively. In forty-six studies of aid recipients compared to nonrecipients, the average effect size was + .132 ($p < .001$). Another way to state this finding is to note that the typical aid recipient has a persistence likelihood five percentage points greater than that of the nonrecipient group. This finding is more impressive when we recall that the basic purpose of financial aid is to equalize opportunity for economically disadvantaged students. Evidence of equalization would be a zero effect size. Other significant findings were that financial aid had a greater effect on persistence (1) in later years than in the freshman year, (2) in two-year colleges than in four-year colleges, (3) in private colleges than in public colleges, and (4) in studies after 1975 than in earlier studies.

Other studies in Murdock's (1990) metanalysis compared groups of recipients with each other rather than with nonrecipients. The principal findings were that (1) men and women were equally affected by financial aid, (2) minority recipients had lower persistence than nonminority recipients, (3) the dollar amount of aid had a significantly positive effect, and (4) scholarships and scholarship and loan combinations had a more positive effect than did loans alone.

St. John (1989) examined the effect of various forms of financial aid on year-to-year student persistence in three large high school graduate cohorts (each approximately four thousand students) who entered college in 1972, 1980, and 1982, respectively. The forms of financial aid studied were grant only, loan only, grant and loan, grant and work, and combination of grant, loan, and work. No form of aid was significantly related to year-to-year persistence for each cohort. However, grant only, grant and loan combinations, and grant, loan, and work combinations were significantly related to year-to-year persistence in a majority of the individual analyses. Loans only were found to be negatively related to persistence in two analyses, positively related in three others, and unrelated in the remaining six. Overall, this study confirmed that financial aid packages are positively associated with year-to-year persistence in college.

Another aspect of financial aid that has been studied is renewability. Woodward (1988) compared the four-year persistence of students who had four-year renewable scholarships to that of students who received single-year scholarships at Boise State University. In two separate samples, the renewable scholarship recipients persisted at significantly higher rates than the single-year recipients.

Several investigators have used sophisticated statistical methods to explore the relationship of financial aid and other variables to persistence. Moline (1987) used path analysis to study the relationship of financial aid and other variables with persistence at a large commuter university. Voorhees (1985) and Nora (1990) used a form of structural equation modeling called LISREL (linear structural relationships) to study the impact of aid on persistence at a major university in the Southwest and among Hispanic community college students. These statistical approaches offer promise because they allow the simultaneous analysis of many variables as well as the decomposition of direct and indirect effects, which helps to clarify the linkages among the variables.

An Institutional Case Study

Virtually all institutions have the opportunity to shape their financial aid policies and practices to some extent. In private colleges, institutionally budgeted scholarship dollars are subject to institutional control. In public colleges, at least the manner in which the various aid components are packaged can be adapted to meet the needs of different students or student groups.

To the extent that institutions can control the amount, type, and makeup of aid packages, these variables are subject to strategic analyses. The basic question, of course, is how can the institution's enrollment objectives be enhanced through the shaping of financial aid policies or practices. Both recruitment and retention strategies are worthy of review and experimentation.

The purpose of this section is to provide examples of how one institution has used institutionally controlled financial aid to affect the recruitment and retention of undergraduate students and how these efforts have been evaluated. The examples are neither unique nor exhaustive. They are, however, illustrative of the kinds of institutional strategies that can be pursued. Subject to the methodological issues raised earlier, attempts were made to evaluate the effectiveness of these strategies.

Scholarship Incentives. In 1987, Rensselaer Polytechnic Institute attempted to increase the enrollment of new freshmen in three of its five schools (Humanities and Social Sciences, Management, and Science) by adjusting the attractiveness of financial aid packages. After all admitted students with demonstrated need were packaged in the normal manner, the packages of students in the three schools were adjusted by increasing the scholarship component of each package by $1,000 and reducing the self-help portion by $1,000. The $1,000 figure was selected because we believed that the net $2,000 "swing" would be enough to make a difference. Thus, a student with a $10,000 need and an original package of $6,500 scholarship and $3,500 self-help instead received a package of $7,500 scholarship and $2,500 self-help. The extra scholarship dollars came from an extra allocation of general institutional funds.

In evaluating the enrollment and financial impact of this strategy, we used the yield (percentage of admitted students who enrolled) experience of 1986 and 1987 as a basis for comparison. In 1986, the yield of admitted freshmen with financial aid in the three schools was 29 percent. Based on the 1987 yield of other students in the class, we estimated that the 1987 yield for the aided students would have been 27 percent without the scholarship incentive. The actual yield for aided students in the three target schools was 33 percent (963 admitted, 317 enrolled). A 27 percent yield would have resulted in 260 enrolled or 57 fewer than actually enrolled.

The goal of increasing freshmen enrollment in the three schools was met. But what were the financial consequences? On the revenue side, the 57 additional students paid tuition of $11,500 for a total of $655,500. On the expense side, we awarded an extra $1,000 to each of the 260 freshmen who presumably would have enrolled anyway for a cost of $260,000. The 57 additional students had an average institutional scholarship of $5,000 for a cost of $285,000. Based on these costs and yield assumptions, the program produced a net revenue of $110,500 in year one.

Because of the success of this strategic initiative, we decided to extend it to all freshmen on aid in 1988. A total of 2,236 freshmen on aid were admitted for 1988. If the yield remained the same as it was in 1987 (30.7 percent), 686 of them would have enrolled. We felt this was a reasonable assumption since the 1988 yield for students not on aid was the same as it had been in 1987. In actuality, 827 (or 37 percent) of the freshmen on aid enrolled, 141 more than would have if yield had remained constant. Financially, the results were also positive:

Revenue:	141 students × $12,250 tuition =	$1,727,250
Expenses:	686 students × $1,000 scholarship =	$686,000
	141 students × $6,000 scholarship =	$846,000
Net:		$195,250

An institution considering an initiative along these lines can calculate ahead of time how many additional students (or, alternatively, how much of a yield increase) it would take to break even. The assumptions of scholarship incentive size and yield increase can be varied to examine the enrollment and financial sensitivity at different levels. The judgment of the admissions director and the financial aid director would seem especially valuable in formulating these assumptions.

Scholarship Matrix

In addition to across-the-board incentives such as just described, more complex variations of the scholarship-to-self-help ratio can also be pursued and evaluated. At Rensselaer we use a packaging matrix that varies the quality of the aid package (that is, the percentage of the package that is scholarship) with the quality and need of the student. The higher the student quality and the lower the student need, the greater the percentage of the package that is scholarship. A simplified version might look like Table 1.

While the wisdom of basing the quality of aid packages on student quality and need can be debated, the point here is that the quality of aid packages can be varied according to whatever student characteristics are seen as most institutionally desirable. Of course, the amount of the package or the extent to which need is met can also be varied. This discussion is in the context of an institutional policy of meeting demonstrated need.

Evaluation of the effectiveness of the strategy depicted in Table 1 requires examination of yield in each of the cells and of assumptions about how changes in scholarship percentage would affect that yield. Following several years of utilizing a matrix similar to that in Table 1 (our operational matrix is actually five-by-five rather than three-by-three), we studied several modifications of the matrix in 1990 to determine their effects on student quality and scholarship expenditures.

We hypothesized that by increasing the scholarship percentage in the high-quality/low-need portion of the scholarship matrix, the upper-left-hand cell, and decreasing the scholarship percentages for the low-quality/high-need portion of the matrix, the lower-right-hand cell, we could accomplish three objectives: (1) maintain overall freshmen enrollment, (2) increase the

Table 1. Sample Financial Aid Packaging Matrix Based on Quality Versus Need of the Student

		Student Admissions Rating		
		High	Middle	Low
Student Need	Low	100	85	70
	Middle	85	70	60
	High	70	60	50

Note: Figures are percentages of scholarship aid within the financial aid packages.

quality of the class as measured by the admissions rating (a global rating emphasizing academic quality), and (3) maintain or reduce institutional scholarship expenditures.

Prior to 1990, our yield experience had taken the form presented in Table 2. We varied the scholarship percentages as described above, adjusted the yields in each cell, and recalculated the number, quality, and scholarship costs of the resulting class summed across the cells. For example, the scholarship percentage in the high-quality/middle-need cell was changed from 85 percent to 100 percent, the yield from 20 percent to 30 percent (an assumption based on our best judgment), and the average scholarship costs for all enrolling students in that cell recalculated. We tried several iterations of this approach in each cell and studied the resultant hypothetical class. We finally selected a new scholarship matrix and await the enrollment results this fall 1991 to evaluate our assumptions.

Reserve Officers' Training Corps (ROTC) Incentive. Within the past three years, institutions with ROTC programs began to offer incentives to ROTC scholarship winners as a recruitment strategy. All three ROTC branches (Army, Air Force, and Marines) offer attractive four-year scholarships that the student can take to whichever school he or she selects from among those offering admission (at Rensselaer, a ROTC scholarship varies from $11,000 to $16,000 in value depending on the type of scholarship). The incentives range from a supplemental grant of a few hundred dollars to free room and board and are almost always offered without regard to need.

In an effort to halt an apparent migration of ROTC scholarship winners to other institutions, we decided to offer a $2,500 renewable no-need scholarship to any ROTC scholarship winner who chose to enroll in 1990. This dollar amount approximates the cost of a residence hall room for the academic year. The results were impressive. Based on our 1989 experience, sixty-five ROTC scholarship winners would have enrolled as freshmen in 1990; with the scholarship incentive, eighty-seven did so.

Since ROTC scholarship winners normally do not qualify for additional financial aid, the evaluation of the financial impact of this new program was straightforward. The extra scholarships cost $217,500, while the extra

Table 2. Rensselaer Pre-1990 Yield Matrix Based on Quality Versus Financial Need of the Student

		Student Admissions Rating		
		High	Middle	Low
Student Need	Low	10	20	30
	Middle	20	30	40
	High	30	40	50

Note: Figures are percentages of admitted students who enrolled.

tuition revenues generated by the additional twenty-two students was $314,600. Since the quality of these students is at least equal to the class as a whole, this was a win-win initiative.

No-Need Scholarships: A Marketing Study. The strategy of experimenting with additional hundreds of thousands or even tens of thousands of scholarship dollars based on assumptions of increased yield has a significant element of risk, especially in today's increasingly competitive market. One way to minimize the risk is to try the new approach on a small subgroup first and observe the results. Another step that can be taken prior to the investment of funds is to ask students how their college choice decisions would have been affected by various scholarship incentives. We had the opportunity to do these hypotheticals as part of a larger marketing study of admitted freshmen in June 1990, just after their college choices had been made. While student responses to what-if questions are not as solid as actual choices, such data can inform decisions about the allocation of scarce scholarships funds.

In telephone interviews with ninety-one admitted freshmen who did not apply for financial aid (presumably those with no need) and who chose to enroll elsewhere, the interviewer asked, "Suppose that Rensselaer had offered you a merit scholarship of $ _____ that was independent of your family's financial need. Would that award have led you to change your choice to Rensselaer?" The amount started at $1,000 and increased at $1,000 increments until the student said the choice would have changed to Rensselaer or until $5,000 was reached. The results are shown in Table 3.

Clearly, as these data indicate, the offer of small merit scholarships to students who can afford a high-cost (approximately $20,000 in 1990) institution is not prudent. As a recruitment strategy, scholarships apparently must be in the $5,000 range, or one-quarter of the annual cost, to make a difference. This finding is consistent with the $4,700 that Chapman and Jackson (1987) found in their multi-institutional study.

For a $5,000 merit scholarship to be cost-effective at our current yield of 33 percent and tuition of $14,300, yield would have to increase to 51

Table 3. Students Who Would Have Chosen Rensselaer Based on Hypothetical Incentive of Merit Scholarships, by Dollar Amount

Amount of Hypothetical Merit Scholarship	N	Cumulative N	Cumulative Percentage
$1,000	—	—	—
$2,000	—	—	—
$3,000	2	2	2.2
$4,000	3	5	5.5
$5,000	10	15	16.5

Note: N = 91.

percent. Since this increase is not a reasonable expectation, we do not intend to implement such a program.

Yield Data. Detailed knowledge of the institutional yield experience is fundamental to any evaluation of the effect of various forms and amounts of financial aid on recruitment of new students. Freshmen (or transfer student) yield should be analyzed in a number of consistent ways each year to have a basis for assessing the impact of any change in financial aid packages.

We have found that yield varies from year to year (plus or minus four percentage points) and systematically varies by curricular area (higher in perceived high-quality areas), by gender (higher among men), by student quality (higher among lower quality), by geography (higher among New York and nearby states), by financial need (higher among higher need), and to a lesser extent by ethnic group (varies across groups).

Other subgroupings may be important at other campuses, such as commuter versus noncommuter, resident versus nonresident, legacy versus nonlegacy, and early decision versus regular decision. All logical student characteristics should be explored. To the extent that student numbers permit, several statistical methods are available to assess the relative effects on yield of membership in various subgroups.

Impact on Retention. Assessment of the impact of financial aid on student retention is at least as complex as assessment in the context of recruitment. For example, Terkla's (1985) model of college persistence includes student demographic characteristics (race, sex, and socioeconomic status), scholastic aptitude, occupational and education goals, institutional characteristics, college academic performance, and financial assistance. Tinto's (1987) retention model is equally complex.

Nevertheless, evaluation of the contribution of financial aid to student persistence is essential, especially given the budget impact of financial aid at most institutions. And given current trends, the budget impact will probably grow not shrink since federal and state aid programs are unlikely to keep pace with college cost increases.

Students often report financial problems as a reason for dropping out of college (Pascarella, 1982). In our exit interviews of students who choose to withdraw (about one-half of the students who leave come in to tell us ahead of time), insufficient finances rank second behind academic matters as the stated cause. In a telephone survey that we conducted with forty-eight freshmen who were eligible to but did not return the following year, lack of finances was the most often cited reason for dropping out.

Of course, financial problems can sometimes serve as a socially acceptable response that obscures a more fundamental reason. In addition, financial problems can also interact with other factors. For example, if satisfaction with one's academic success or personal life is lacking, the cost of the college may be viewed as too high even if the student can "afford" it. How much one is willing to sacrifice financially is a function of the other benefits experienced or expected later. Student interviews or survey research can provide insight and some useful data. Student behavior can provide more objective information, although it too presents problems of interpretation.

An opportunity to study the impact of financial aid on retention exists when a significant change occurs in the amount or form of aid to continuing students. An institutional example is our change in 1989 in the allocation of institutional scholarship dollars to continuing students. A long-standing policy of reducing institutional scholarships for students with low grades the previous year was abolished and, through a significant increase in the scholarship budget, replaced by a commitment to maintain scholarship levels from year to year. Under the old policy, several hundred students each year received scholarship reductions if their grades for the previous year fell below a preannounced level.

In the first year, we calculated that an increase in our normal year-to-year retention rates of 1.15 percent in each class, or forty-five students overall, would offset the additional institutional scholarship allocation required by the new policy. The result was that we enrolled forty-two students more than our normal retention rate would have predicted. We continued the policy in 1990 and will do a more careful study that examines retention among aid recipients in various categories defined by grade point averages.

This example underscores the importance of maintaining historical retention data as a basis for comparison. Just as yield data are critical for assessing recruitment strategies, retention data are necessary for evaluating retention strategies. As with yield data, retention data should be available for various curricular and demographic subgroups and should be analyzed with respect to the amount and form of financial aid and the extent to which need is met.

Conclusion

A variety of national trends have converged to cast a spotlight on student financial aid. The decline in high school graduates and resultant competition among colleges, the failure of federal and state financial aid programs to keep pace with college costs, the growing gap between disposable family income and college costs, and the increasing difficulty of balancing institutional budgets have each contributed to the increased attention being given to financial aid in enrollment management.

Institutions have responded with many new approaches to offering financial aid to admitted students and to packaging aid for continuing students. While institutional missions, goals, and resources vary widely, nearly all institutions can assess the impact of financial aid and make strategic decisions on this basis to advance enrollment objectives.

Such assessment is complicated by the existence of multiple variables that are known to affect student enrollment behavior and by the inherent difficulty of identifying appropriate control groups. Nevertheless, considerable literature exists in both multi-institutional and single institutional contexts on the impact of financial aid (Fenske, 1989).

Both need-based and non–need-based aid have been shown to be effective in recruiting students in a variety of settings. For students with need, financial aid appears to offset variations in college costs that affect their enrollment decisions. No-need scholarships are less uniformly effective and careful study of the net financial impact on the institution is essential. The perceived renewability of aid also has been shown to be an important factor.

Financial aid has a positive effect on student retention in a variety of college settings. Several different forms and combinations of aid have been shown to enhance persistence, although the evidence of loans alone has been mixed. Aid needs to be studied in combination with other factors known to influence retention.

Evaluation of the impact of financial aid on recruitment or retention requires careful specification of institutional goals and, in some cases, of the relative priority of quality, quantity, diversity, and cost. It also requires a rich set of historical data on yield and retention of previous student cohorts. New statistical techniques, notably path analysis and LISREL, offer promise in sorting out the linkages among the many variables involved in student enrollment behavior.

Institutional self-interest and national trends point to the critical need for more careful study of the impact of financial aid on recruitment and retention. The need exists and the tools exist. The rest is up to us.

References

Anderson, C. H., Ellickson, K., Nuetzel, J., and White, G. W. "The Uses of Institutional Financial Aid as a Marketing Incentive in Higher Education." *Journal of Student Financial Aid*, 1985, *15*, 19–30.

Chapman, R. G., and Jackson, R. *College Choices of Academically Able Students: The Influence of No-Need Financial Aid and Other Factors*. New York: College Board, 1987.

College Board. *Trends in Student Aid: 1980 to 1990*. Washington, D.C.: College Board, 1990.

Fenske, R. H. (ed.). *Studying the Impact of Student Aid on Institutions*. New Directions for Institutional Research, no. 62. San Francisco: Jossey-Bass, 1989.

Hossler, D. *Enrollment Management: An Integrated Approach*. New York: College Board, 1984.

Huff, R. P. "Collaboration Between Institutional Researchers and Student Financial Aid Officers in Developing Student Persistence Policy." In R. H. Fenske (ed.), *Studying the Impact of Student Aid on Institutions*. New Directions for Institutional Research, no. 62. San Francisco: Jossey-Bass, 1989.

Iba, D. L., Simpson, D. B., and Stockburger, D. W. "The Effectiveness of No-Need Scholarships in Recruiting Students." *College and University*, 1988, *63*, 263–272.

Moline, A. E. "Financial Aid and Student Persistence: An Application of Causal Modeling." *Research in Higher Education*, 1987, *26*, 130–147.

Murdock, T. A. "Financial Aid and Persistence: An Integrative Review of the Literature." *NASPA Journal*, 1990, *27*, 213–221.

Nora, A. "Campus-Based Aid Programs as Determinants of Retention Among Hispanic Community College Students." *Journal of Higher Education*, 1990, *61*, 312–331.

Pascarella, E. T. (ed.). *Studying Student Attrition.* New Directions for Institutional Research, no. 36. San Francisco: Jossey-Bass, 1982.

Porter, J. D., and Barberini, P. G. "Collaboration Between Institutional Researchers and Student Financial Aid Officers in Developing Student Persistence Policy." In R. H. Fenske (ed.), *Studying the Impact of Student Aid on Institutions.* New Directions for Institutional Research, no. 62. San Francisco: Jossey-Bass, 1989.

St. John, E. P. "The Influence of Student Aid on Persistence." *Journal of Student Financial Aid*, 1989, *19*, 52–68.

Terkla, D. G. "Does Financial Aid Enhance Undergraduate Persistence?" *Journal of Student Financial Aid*, 1985, *15*, 11–18.

Tinto, V. *Leaving College: Rethinking the Causes and Cures of Student Attrition.* Chicago: University of Chicago Press, 1987.

Voorhees, R. A. "Student Finances and Campus-Based Financial Aid: A Structural Model Analysis of the Persistence of High-Need Freshmen." *Research in Higher Education*, 1985, *22*, 65–92.

Woodward, C. "The Effects of Single-Year Scholarships Versus Renewable Scholarships on Student Persistence." *College and University*, 1988, *63*, 162–167.

Zelenak, B., and Cockriel, I. W. "Who Benefits from No-Need Scholarships?" *Journal of Student Financial Aid*, 1986, *16*, 20–26.

Lee Wilcox is vice-president for student affairs at Rensselaer Polytechnic Institute, Troy, New York, a position he has held since 1979. He previously served as director of admissions at the University of Wisconsin, Madison.

The key to tracking and evaluating the academic progress of students, particularly at complex institutions, is the development of a student-tracking system with the flexibility to support a diverse community of users and applications.

Tracking Academic Progress Within a Complex Academic Environment

Richard D. Howard, Brenda H. Rogers

An important indicator of the success of colleges and universities in achieving their missions is degree completion, both at the undergraduate and graduate levels. To external agencies and the public, overall retention and graduation rates often are accepted as appropriate measures of institutional effectiveness. In general, institutional retention and graduation rates probably belong on the list of reasonable indicators of institutional effectiveness at smaller undergraduate liberal arts colleges where the curriculum is largely the same for all students. However, as the size of the student body grows and the complexity of academic offerings increases, overall retention and graduation statistics are less useful than are retention and graduation rates of specific subgroups of students. Under these circumstances, the overall statistics are more effectively used as norms against which retention and graduation rates of subgroups of students who have participated in specific intervention programs and have similar academic or nonacademic experiences can be compared for the purpose of evaluating the success of these programs.

In this chapter, methods of evaluating student retention to graduation at medium-sized to large, complex universities are explored. While this environment defines the frame of reference of the discussion, the techniques described are transferable to any size or type of institution. In most instances, as the size and complexity of the institution decrease, less effort and fewer data-related resources are necessary to support retention and graduation studies. We do not attempt to present a discussion of traditional evaluation techniques nor do we discuss the merits of various retention intervention strategies. Instead, our intent is to define relevant retention issues for complex institutions and to discuss the development and characteristics of a retention system that can be used as a base for evaluating the academic progress of specific student subgroups and the efficiency and effectiveness of academic and nonacademic programs. Actual examples drawn from universities with complex academic programs illustrate how such a retention system assists in evaluating academic and nonacademic programs and policies.

The general mission and goals of a university appropriately serve as the primary parameters for analysis of retention and graduation patterns. However, as mentioned above, overall graduation and retention statistics are of limited value to the analysis of the retention patterns of specific groups of students or students in specific academic and nonacademic programs. One of the basic principles described by Ewell (1987) for an integrated research program to support enrollment management and retention studies is disaggregation of the data by subgroups of students who may have different behavioral patterns. As such, the design of a system to monitor retention patterns and graduation rates must have the flexibility to allow examination of the academic progress of specific subgroups of students both by the management and leadership of the institution and by program directors and faculty groups.

Implicit in the above statement is the notion of a centrally created and maintained computerized longitudinal tracking system. This system may be a single file or a series of integrated files, extended, often by necessity, to other operational data bases maintained by central administrative and student support units. Regardless of its structure, the purpose of the system is to record the academic status of students at specific points in time throughout their academic careers. In this chapter we focus on important considerations for the efficient maintenance and effective utilization of a centralized longitudinal tracking system at a complex institution (see Ewell, 1987, for a discussion of the general design and construction of a longitudinal tracking system).

Data Base Development and Management

As a primary tool in the evaluation of retention and graduation patterns, the utility of a longitudinal tracking system is directly defined by its ability to map various subgroups of students through the academic programs offered by the college or university. As such, the complexity of the system is directly related to the diversity and number of academic programs and the size of the student population. The number and diversity of its potential users is another challenge to the utility of the system; that is, the more complex the system, the more difficult its direct use by evaluators and decision makers across the campus. The key is to develop a longitudinal tracking system with the flexibility to identify specific cohorts or subgroups of students and to provide an electronic environment that readily allows easy tracking and analysis of their academic progress. The following discussion explores several critical factors in the development and maintenance of a system that meets the criterion of flexibility in the examination of subgroups of students and in the distribution of the data to a wide range of users.

Integration with Other Institutional Data Bases. The ability to link the longitudinal tracking system with other operating systems of the university (admissions, enrollment, financial aid, and so on) is essential. In general, the linkage is accomplished by assigning a unique identifier (usually the Social Security number) to each student, and the identifier becomes a part of his or her record in every institutional data base or file in which information about the student is stored. As such, the key element that links the individual student records in the longitudinal tracking system to other data bases is this common student identifier.

The ability to integrate the longitudinal system with other operating data bases has two important implications. First, many academic and demographic characteristics of the students do not need to be maintained in the longitudinal tracking system, since they can be accessed from other institutional data bases. Used as independent variables in evaluation studies, this information can be merged with the tracking system to serve as the parameters for identifying the particular cohort to be studied.

Second, the academic status of each student in a longitudinal tracking system must be updated periodically. Usually the registrar initially records academic status in central institutional data bases. These files are the source of data for the longitudinal tracking system. A unique student identifier facilitates the transfer of the data from data bases containing the students' official records to the longitudinal tracking system. Once the specific parameters of the data transfer have been developed, the process can become a routine data-processing function, occurring automatically at each scheduled update.

Evaluation studies often need to relate retention and graduation patterns to data collected from or about subgroups of students. These data are usually collected in the form of surveys (at new-student orientations, from alumni or employers, and so on) interviews (exit interviews or focus interviews), or scores on admissions or placement tests. Terenzini (1987) provides an informative discussion of the basic terms, concepts, and problems encountered in studying attrition and retention using these types of data sources. Important in the collection of these data is that the responses can be tied to a unique student identifier. This linkage is needed to study relationships between survey responses and other externally collected data and the academic progression and graduation patterns of the students.

Decentralized Use of the Longitudinal Tracking System. The utility of a longitudinal tracking system at a large institution is in part a function of its accessibility to users across campus. Specifically, users of the system must be able to identify specific student cohorts, interface or link the system with other institutional or specially created data bases, and manipulate the resulting data set to create reliable and valid information. The present state of computer hardware and software technology allows the system to be easily accessed with common statistical packages (for example, SAS and SPSS) and, if desired, down-loading to micro-based statistical packages and spreadsheet or data base applications (see Howard, McLaughlin, and McLaughlin, 1989, for a discussion of data quality in a decentralized environment).

Defining Appropriate Cohorts. Depending on the size and complexity of the student population, the institution may decide to maintain separate files for distinct cohorts of students entering at one point in time (for example, freshmen, transfers, graduate students, professional students, nondegree students); or the institution may decide to develop a single file for all new students entering each term or year. The particular architecture of the file is dependent in large part on the technical capabilities available at the institution. Therefore, technical experts at the computer center should be consulted when designing the system. Several issues to be considered include the staff support available for creating and maintaining the files and for documenting the process, the computer time required to process the files, the distribution of the data to users via the computer network, and the technical ability in the institutional research office to manipulate the files.

If a single large file is chosen, then all identifying variables needed to request separate retention reports are usually included in each student record. Enrollment status, such as new freshman, new transfer, or new graduate student, is an essential variable for inclusion on a single file.

At a university with many diverse academic programs, a longitudinal tracking system may consist of several separate files reflecting different categories or cohorts of students. At a minimum, separate files for cohorts of first-time freshmen, new transfers from other institutions, and newly admitted graduate and professional students should be created. In line with the above discussion, the size and complexity of the institution should dictate the number of individual files created. Initially, student cohorts are defined by type of student and the time of initial entry into the institution. Cohorts of new students should be identified either at the beginning of each academic term or only at the beginning of the fall term. At this time, data from the admissions' files or the registrar's files should be extracted for the longitudinal system. Ewell (1987) discusses the use of census files or dynamic operating files as the source of data for populating the longitudinal file(s).

The decision whether to identify cohorts every term or only once each academic year depends primarily on the number of new students enrolled each term. Universities with traditional undergraduate admissions patterns admit the majority of new undergraduates for the fall term, with relatively small numbers of new freshmen enrolling during winter or spring terms. However, many new freshmen may enroll during the summer prior to their first fall term. Institutions should include these new freshmen with their fall cohorts in the longitudinal tracking system, a practice consistent with federal definitions for reporting new freshmen. The academic activity of these students during the preceding summer should be distinguishable from their activity during regular terms as it could become an important factor in studies of time to graduation. Universities with flexible admissions policies may have large numbers of students, both at the graduate and undergraduate levels, enrolling as new students each term. These institutions must then define new cohorts of students each term in the tracking system.

The tracking files must distinguish new transfer and graduate students. If fairly large numbers of new transfer and graduate students enroll in terms other than the fall, separate term cohorts must be established for these students.

Institutions with large numbers of nondegree students who may eventually apply to and be accepted into degree programs may need to monitor the retention of these students. Separate tracking files for new nondegree students may be created and maintained in the same fashion as used for traditional degree-seeking students. However, when these students move into degree programs, their classification in the longitudinal tracking system and in subsequent retention studies becomes problematic. Are they continuing students or transfer students? The initial design of the system must resolve this important issue.

Graduate and professional students are admitted into specific programs. Typically, if these students change programs, they must apply to and be admitted into the new programs. They should, therefore, be treated as "new" students in these programs. Thus, a graduate student who moves from education to psychology may appear as a drop-out from education and be identified as a new graduate student in psychology in a subsequent tracking file.

Institutions may have special evening degree programs in which all students are part-time. Such students should be identified and tracked separately from traditional degree students. Even with no policies regarding part-time status, universities with separate evening colleges or other programs designed for part-time students must either include a variable distinguishing these students from day students on the tracking files or else create separate tracking files for the evening students. The retention and graduation patterns of evening students may differ from those of traditional students and therefore merit independent study, especially if the programs involved are an important component of the academic offerings of the institution.

Variables Maintained in the Longitudinal Tracking System. The variables maintained in the longitudinal tracking system fall into two major categories. The first group consists of fixed variables, located in the root segment of the file and extracted for all students in the system. These variables usually are descriptive, identifying demographic and academic characteristics of each student at entry into the institution. The variables are static and do not change during the student's time at the institution while in a particular student status. If a student changes status (for example, from undergraduate status to graduate or professional status), then a new cohort file contains this student along with a new root segment that reflects demographic or academic changes that have occurred since the student initially entered the university. Inclusion of a variable in the root segment should, in part, be based on the importance of that variable to the evaluation of academic progress. As discussed above, the one variable on the root segment that is not optional is the student identifier.

Demographic variables commonly found in the root segment include gender, race and ethnicity, birthdate, residence, and citizenship. The choices of which demographic variables to include in the root segment should be a function of the mission of the institution and the clientele it serves. For instance, public institutions, with their commitment to serving the citizens of a state, or even specific counties within the state, may be particularly interested in monitoring their successes in retaining and graduating resident students.

Academic variables in the root segment are primarily those used in the admissions process. These variables might include scores on admission tests (Scholastic Aptitude Test or American College Test), high school grade point average, high school rank, admissions index (when calculated), and major area of study (when identified). In addition, ratings of noncognitive variables (leadership, parental support for education, motivation to complete college, and so on) might be included if they are critical components of the admissions process. Such information allows the institution to test the validity of the admissions criteria against future performance, as measured by grades earned in college, retention, and graduation rates.

The second group of variables in the longitudinal tracking system are those that define the academic status of the student at specific points in time during the academic year. At each update of the tracking system, the same variables that define the academic status of the student are copied from the registrar's files to the files in the tracking system. Typically, the variables include major, total hours attempted, total hours passed, cumulative grade point average, academic standing (suspended, academic warning, or good standing), and graduation status. These variables collected at consistent points within the academic calendar of the institution facilitate the identification of patterns about students' progress through academic programs and the time that students take to complete degree requirements.

Updating the Longitudinal Tracking System. After the initial cohort files are created, data on each student are extracted for each term or year at consistent points over an established time period. The number of years over which students are tracked depends on institutional policies. For example, a university requiring master's degree students to complete the program within a seven-year period would design its tracking files to monitor master's cohorts for seven years. On the other hand, there may be no policy regarding time to complete an undergraduate program. In this case an analysis of time taken to complete an undergraduate degree might indicate that, beyond seven years, increases in graduation rates are negligible. Therefore, a decision to track undergraduate cohorts through seven years would seem reasonable.

Another decision to be made at the design stage of a longitudinal tracking system is how often during the academic year to update the system. In some cases, once at the beginning of the fall term may be adequate. However, at a complex institution where students frequently change academic majors, an updating of the system at the beginning or end of each term might be more appropriate.

Structure of the Tracking Files. Lolli (this volume) discusses many elements to consider in the development of a longitudinal tracking system. At risk of redundancy, we want to emphasize that as the institution increases in size, the number of constituents whose diverse interests and needs are pertinent to a student tracking system also increases. As mentioned earlier, the distribution of data within the system should serve the needs of the institution at large as well as the specific units that want to conduct their own analyses of retention. Assuming security requirements have been met, a trade-off must be made between the complexity of the data configuration in the system and the ease with which users can access and analyze the data. Obviously, the more complex the system, the more central support from the office of institutional research is essential to effective decentralized access and data analysis. On the other hand, complex data configurations tend to require less storage on the computer and thus are often the choice of data-processing personnel. Staff from the institutional research office and computer center typically need to negotiate the final structure of the tracking files. While institutional researchers should settle for nothing less than what is needed to track the academic progress of students via common analytical software, it is often the systems' analysts and programmers in the computing center who write the programs to create and update the system as well as ensure that the updates occur as scheduled.

As Lolli notes, there are trade-offs in the development of a longitudinal student-tracking system, so users should be prepared to negotiate all aspects of the system's development. What should not be negotiable is the update schedule. If this schedule is not consistent with the academic calendar of the institution or is not strictly followed, lack of data reliability can make comparisons from year-to-year or even from one academic term to the next invalid.

Interpretation of Retention and Graduation Statistics

The primary purpose of a longitudinal tracking system is to support the computation of graduation and retention statistics; for example, the retention rate of a particular freshman class at the beginning of its second year can be defined as the percentage of the total cohort that returned one calendar year after entering the institution. However, an average of several cohorts may provide a better picture of the institution's overall effectiveness in retaining freshmen. On the other hand, if the purpose of a tracking system is to determine whether retention efforts focused on the freshman year are having an impact, comparison of several cohorts may provide useful trend data. The ability to examine trend data is our first step toward evaluating institutional retention efforts.

Obviously, students who are continuously enrolled should graduate earlier than students who stop-out. It may be important to compare graduation statistics for those who are continuously enrolled with those who have withdrawn for one or more terms. Reports of overall retention and graduation rates typically retain the students who have withdrawn for one or more terms. Their inclusion or exclusion from graduation statistics should be clearly explained.

Students who are suspended by the institution for one or more terms should constitute a separate category for reporting purposes. These students should be retained in the cohort, but in a unique category separate from those reported as enrolled, withdrawn, or graduated. If the calculations of retention and graduation rates remove these or any other category of students, the reports must describe the procedures clearly.

Institutions may also choose to exclude other subgroups of students when reporting retention and graduation rates. For instance, institutions may exclude those students who have been admitted as exceptions to the normal admissions process or criteria, particularly when the purpose is to evaluate the effectiveness of admissions criteria (although the retention of admissions exceptions should be carefully tracked). Comparisons of retention rates for subgroups of students may be the most useful information derived from a longitudinal student-tracking system, especially to units responsible for academic programs and student support services.

Comparisons of retention and graduation rates between institutions is problematic because institutions differ in their educational philosophies and missions. Institutions with an open-door admissions policy, whose mission is to provide educational opportunity to all applicants within a certain region or who have certain characteristics, will probably have retention and graduation rates different from those of colleges and universities with selective admissions standards. Institutions that serve adult and non-traditional students will have retention and graduation rates different from those of institutions that serve the traditional college-aged population.

Other characteristics of institutions may relate to retention and graduation rates. Universities with a large proportion of residential students probably have higher retention and graduation rates than those of universities serving a commuting population. Another factor related to lower retention rates is the frequency of students working full-time off-campus (Astin, 1975). On the other hand, students who work on-campus tend to have higher retention rates than those of other students. The financial need of students, the availability of financial aid, and the type of financial aid packages available are factors affecting retention. Universities with large numbers of students who need financial support but who do not have all of their financial needs met probably have lower retention rates than those of universities with a lower proportion of students in need of financial aid. Again, it must be stressed that in order to study the relationships of student retention and attrition to institutional characteristics, variables must be identified that define the specific institutional characteristics in relationship to the student. These variables then define the parameters for tracking subgroups of students.

In summary, retention and graduation rates should be interpreted in the light of the mission of the university and the characteristics of its students. In fact, the mission of the institution should guide the selection of variables for inclusion in the tracking system. Although overall retention and graduation statistics may provide a global picture of the university's effectiveness in retaining and graduating its students, statistics reported separately for subgroups of students are much more meaningful, especially for internal policy decisions. Although national statistics on average retention and graduation rates may be helpful in interpreting overall institutional statistics, comparisons with peer institutions, that is, institutions with similar students and missions, are more informative. The purpose of the comparison should guide the selection of a comparison group (Teeter and Brinkman, 1987). Because of differences in institutional policies and practices, the best use of retention and graduation statistics may be for the internal evaluation of policies, programs, and procedures.

Examples of Using a Student-Tracking System for Evaluation

With solid student data bases in place colleges and universities are in a position to conduct extensive studies of student retention. The following examples illustrate the use of centrally developed, longitudinal tracking systems. The intent is to illustrate the use of these systems to address questions about specific cohorts or subgroups of students.

Example 1. A university that serves a large number of local students may find that a significant proportion of new students never intend to graduate from the institution. Their intent is to accumulate credits that can be transferred to other institutions that offer degree programs of their choice, or that are perceived to be more prestigious. Table 1 presents graduation rates from a comprehensive university located in an urban area with several outstanding universities within commuting distance. The data are organized by student intention (based on responses to an entering freshman survey) to graduate or to transfer from the university (Rogers and Pratt, 1989). Those freshmen who expressed the goal of graduating from this university were twice as likely to have graduated in five years than were those who intended to transfer to other institutions.

In this example, the data collected from a specific student survey were linked, by a common student identifier, to the institution's longitudinal tracking system to develop information about the relationship of students' initial intent to graduate and their actual graduation rates. Upon identifying student intent, institutions are able to more specifically target their retention intervention programs. In this case, it is possible that two types of intervention programs will emerge. One set of programs might be directed at students who plan to graduate, a group that institutions should least want to lose. A second set of programs might attempt to convert planned withdrawals to goal-oriented persisters.

Example 2. The overall four-year graduation rates had been declining steadily at a large, public university. The Office of Institutional Research was asked to study the decline and identify reasons for it. A survey of recent graduates, combined with tracking files, allowed the comparison of subgroups of students (Wolfe and Rogers, 1986). One factor identified in survey responses of the graduates as significantly related to the increased time to graduation was the changing of majors. The study found that for a sample of recent graduates, 57 percent of the students who had changed majors took more than five years to graduate, as compared to 37 percent who did not change majors while enrolled at the university. Furthermore, in response to an open-ended survey question about the reasons students

Table 1. Comparison of Four- and Five-Year Graduation Rates Based on Intentions of 1982 Entering Freshmen

	Four-Year Rates			Five-Year Rates		
Intention	Enrolled	Graduated	Withdrew	Enrolled	Graduated	Withdrew
Graduate	36.0	16.8	47.2	14.3	33.7	52.0
Transfer	19.2	10.3	70.5	.2	16.9	77.9

Note: Figures are percentages.

Source: Rogers and Pratt, 1989.

took more than four years to graduate, 21 percent identified their changes in majors as a factor.

Analysis of correlations between the number of years needed to graduate and the academic school from which the students graduated led to the conclusion that students in the technical and scientific programs were more likely to have difficulty completing in four years if they changed majors than if they had initially enrolled in those programs. In the School of Forest Resources program, 79 percent of those who had not changed majors graduated in four years, as compared to only 22 percent of those who had changed majors and eventually graduated in forest resources. In the School of Textiles, the four-year graduation rates were 72 percent for those not changing majors, and only 33 percent for those who had changed their majors within the textile programs.

The conclusion from this study of graduation rates and changes of major was that the more structured and technical the program, the more likely a change in major would lead to increased time to graduate. Programs with few electives, tight sequencing of courses, and relatively little overlap with programs outside of their schools required students to enroll as freshmen and persist in the major if they expected to graduate in four years. This finding led to the question of whether a core curriculum or a general education program common to all undergraduates, regardless of their majors, was desirable, especially since other studies had found that approximately one-half of entering freshmen changed their majors at least once.

This is an intriguing example of how retention data can illuminate the interaction effects of curricular issues and the educational experiences of students. In this instance, retention data played a role in the review of general education requirements at this institution.

Example 3. A major, public research university has developed a new program for entering freshmen to increase the retention and graduation rates of the institution's undergraduates. The Residential Learning Program attracted a volunteer group of new freshmen who all live in the same residence hall. Through increased involvement of students in campus life and increased interaction with staff, faculty, and other students, program planners at present expect a higher retention rate for these freshmen after their first year than is expected for other freshmen. Because students volunteered for the program rather than being selected at random for participation, the evaluation requires a comparison group that matches (academically and demographically) the characteristics of the experimental group. Over the next five or six years the evaluators plan to compare the retention patterns of the two groups through analyses supported by the institution's longitudinal tracking system. If the students in the Residential Learning Program have higher retention and graduation rates than those of the comparison group, the evaluation will support the continuation of the program, at least for self-selecting populations. In the long run, the results may influence resource allocations for student life programs at this institution.

The examples discussed above reflect typical uses of a longitudinal tracking system. Other uses of the system to track specific student populations include evaluation of the academic progress of athletes in support of advising, certification documentation, and National Collegiate Athletic Association reporting mandates; evaluation of the effects on student performance of an experimental sequencing of two required English courses; and evaluation of graduation rates of students of different ethnic origins.

A longitudinal tracking system that is linked to operational data bases and specially created data bases can support the evaluation of retention and graduation patterns for a variety of purposes. The key, particularly at complex institutions, is to design into the system the flexibility to support a diverse community of users and applications.

References

Astin, A. W. *Preventing Students from Dropping Out: A Longitudinal, Multi-Institutional Study of College Dropouts.* San Francisco: Jossey-Bass, 1975.

Ewell, P. T. "Principles of Longitudinal Enrollment Analysis: Conducting Retention and Student Flow Studies." In J. Muffo and G. W. McLaughlin (eds.), *A Primer on Institutional Research.* Tallahassee, Fla.: Association for Institutional Research, 1987.

Howard, R. D., McLaughlin, G. W., and McLaughlin, J. S. "Bridging the Gap Between the Data Base and User in a Distributed Environment." *Cause/Effect,* 1989, *12* (2), 19-25.

Rogers, B. H., and Pratt, L. K. "The Relationship of Freshmen's Intentions, Motivations, Academic Aptitude, and College Performance to Persistence in College." Paper presented at the annual forum of the Association for Institutional Research, Baltimore, Maryland, May 1, 1989.

Teeter, D. J., and Brinkman, P. T. "Peer Institutional Studies/Institutional Comparisons." In J. Muffo and G. W. McLaughlin (eds.), *A Primer on Institutional Research.* Tallahassee, Fla.: Association for Institutional Research, 1987.

Terenzini, P. T. "Studying Student Attrition and Retention." In J. Muffo and G. W. McLaughlin (eds.), *A Primer on Institutional Research.* Tallahassee, Fla.: Association for Institutional Research, 1987.

Wolfe, K. L., and Rogers, B. H. "Factors Related to the Declining Four-Year Graduation Rates." Paper presented at the annual meeting of the Southern Association for Institutional Research and the Society of College and University Planning, Pipestem, West Virginia, October 15, 1986.

Richard D. Howard is director of the Office of Institutional Research at North Carolina State University, Raleigh, and serves on the executive committee of the Association for Institutional Research.

Brenda H. Rogers is associate director of the Office of Research, Evaluation, and Planning at North Carolina Central University, Durham, and is president of the Southern Association for Institutional Research for 1990–1991.

Community colleges need to adopt a broad conceptual definition of a continuing student in the design and evaluation of their retention strategies. This chapter presents such a definition and an evaluation plan for a marketing activity based on the new definition.

Evaluating Retention-Driven Marketing in a Community College: An Alternative Approach

Richard Tichenor, John J. Cosgrove

Student retention is a major concern of educational institutions for a number of reasons that transcend enrollment totals, but it is also a vital component of marketing strategies. If marketing is successful and increases the client base of an institution, it must address the retention of existing clients as well as the recruitment of new clients. The importance of student retention has become increasingly apparent to institutions in recent years. As the segments of the population that comprise the traditional sources of new students continue to decline in size, more attention is being given to retention as a marketing activity. As the term is used in this chapter, retention-driven marketing refers to activities that encourage students to re-enroll in order to complete their educational goals.

The size of the traditional student population affects four-year institutions to a greater extent than it does community colleges, which typically serve large numbers of nontraditional students. For this and other reasons, most retention-driven marketing strategies have been initially developed in the context of four-year institutions. As community colleges began to increase their efforts in retention-based marketing, they often adopted the definitions, premises, and methods of the four-year schools.

The four-year retention strategies are directed toward increasing the number of students who pursue their degrees through consecutive semesters of enrollment. The methods by which this marketing goal is pursued typically borrow concepts from Tinto's (1975, 1987) model of student attrition. The basic premises appear sound: Once students enroll, make sure that they re-enroll each semester by increasing their academic and social integration into the college until they complete their degrees.

Like many other community colleges, Saint Louis Community College, a multi-campus system, has embraced aspects of the Tinto model in designing a variety of programs aimed at increasing the percentages of fall students who re-enroll for the spring semester. These programs are similar to those designed at other urban community colleges insofar as they focus on increased student services related to advising and counseling, academic support, academic early warning systems, new-student orientation, and increased student activities. The college also experimented with mailed invitations that encouraged fall students to re-enroll for the spring.

Despite these activities, an examination of fall-to-spring retention rates for the past six years reveals that there has not been a significant increase in these rates. Since 1984, the average percentage of fall students who re-enroll for the spring has been 61 percent, ranging from a low of 59.8 percent to a high of 62.8 percent. Borrowing from the work of Pascarella, Duby, and Iverson (1983), the college also investigated the impact of student background characteristics on fall-to-spring retention rates. This investigation revealed important differences between several background subsets: full-time students were more likely to re-enroll than were part-time students, white students were more likely to re-enroll than were nonwhite students, and students intending to earn a degree were more likely to re-enroll than were those without such an intention. But a historical review of fall-to-spring retention rates revealed that there were not significant increases within any student subsets over time.

These findings have led the college to more closely examine the reasons why fall students do not re-enroll for the spring semester, and the likelihood that they will re-enroll at a later date. Those examinations underscored the need for a broader definition of "continuing student" than was previously used. The broader definition, in turn, pointed to the need to expand retention strategies and evaluation. This chapter reviews these examinations, describes an expanded strategy, presents an initial evaluation of that strategy, and discusses directions for further development of the strategy and its evaluation.

Review of Previous Findings at Saint Louis Community College

In order to save time and increase the efficiency of our work, we reviewed related studies conducted at Saint Louis Community College.

Many of the Fall Students Who Did Not Re-Enroll in the Spring Had Achieved Their Educational Goals. The question of why fall students do not re-enroll for the spring semester has been most directly addressed by periodically surveying random samples of students who did not re-enroll. The findings of those surveys consistently suggest that a substantial number of these students are success stories rather than retention problems. Approximately one-half of Saint Louis Community College students have nondegree educational goals (credit for transfer to a four-year institution, nondegree career training, improvement of an existing job skill, or increased knowledge in an area of personal interest). In each of the two most recent surveys 27 percent of the respondents indicated that they did not re-enroll for the spring semester because they had successfully completed their educational goals in the fall semester.

The Majority Who Did Not Complete Their Educational Goals in the Fall and Did Not Re-Enroll for Spring Had Reasons Largely Unrelated to Factors Controlled by the College. The majority of reasons for not returning in the spring cited by survey respondents who had not achieved their goals were personal in nature (other demands on their time, job conflicts, and so on). These are factors over which the college can exert little influence. The vast majority of these respondents also rated Saint Louis Community College as either a good or excellent institution for students who share their educational goals, an additional indication that most students do not leave due to institutional failure to address their needs.

Most Fall Students Who Did Not Re-Enroll for Spring Planned to Re-Enroll at a Later Date. About 62 percent of the respondents in recent surveys have indicated that they did not achieve their educational goals, but that they planned to re-enroll at a later date. About one-half of these respondents, or roughly 31 percent, planned to re-enroll in the following fall semester.

Many Students Who Appeared to Be Retention Problems When Retention Was Evaluated on a Consecutive-Semester Basis Did in Fact Re-Enroll at a Later Date. An examination of the composition of fall enrollments at Saint Louis Community College with respect to student entry status provided one indication of the magnitude of the stop-out phenomenon. For the three consecutive fall semesters of 1987 to 1989 an average of 6,117 students were re-entry students, that is, they had been away from college for at least one semester. These students typically account for about 20 percent of total fall enrollment.

Examinations of return rates after one semester of absence have found 16–17 percent of the fall students who do not graduate and do not re-enroll for the spring semester return the following fall semester. Many additional students miss more than one semester but still return.

Evidence that stop-out behavior is common among students who eventually achieve their educational goals was provided by an examination of attendance patterns of associate degree graduates. Fewer than one in five completed the degree in two years, and the median number of semesters between first entry and degree completion was nine semesters, due to a combination of stop-out and part-time attendance.

A Broader View of Retention

The brief overview of student behavior summarized above is no doubt familiar to all readers who work in community college systems. Most have observed and studied the same factors in their own institutions. The prevalence of nondegree goals and stop-out behavior clearly complicate retention efforts and studies in the community college. The broader definition of continuing student that we propose does not eliminate those complications, but it does cast them in a slightly different light. In that light, new challenges and opportunities for retention strategies and evaluations are more obvious.

Our broader definition of continuing student, which is especially appropriate in the community college context, is the following: One who persists in the pursuit of a degree or nondegree educational goal either through attendance in consecutive semesters or through intermittent attendance with a definite intent to return and continued commitment to the goal during semesters of nonattendance. This definition cannot be used for precise quantification of continuing students, but it does provide an improved conceptual framework for development and evaluation of retention-driven marketing strategies.

Implications for Retention Strategies and Evaluation

One of the implications of this new definition of continuing student is that most evaluations understate retention rates by counting all nonreturning nongraduates as dropouts. Those nonreturning students who have achieved nondegree educational goals are the nondegree counterparts of graduates. Like graduates, they clearly should not be included in evaluations of retention efforts. Stop-outs should be included but, in our view, should be regarded as retention effort successes rather than failures. For instance, the fact that a student stops-out does not mean that efforts aimed at academic and social integration have failed. To the contrary, a continued commitment to college attendance when external demands interrupt enrollment suggests that integration has been achieved.

A determination of what percentages of nonreturning nongraduates are nondegree goal achievers, stop-outs, and true dropouts is not without its problems, of course. The typical retention study must be supplemented with a survey of nonreturning nongraduates regarding goal achievement and intent to return, and with tracking of actual re-enrollment of stop-outs in future semesters. If the researcher is asked to provide "answers" before this more complete evaluation is possible, it is important that the nature of the more limited findings is explicitly noted.

The implications are not limited to questions of who should be counted in retention evaluations, however. The broader definition also implies that retention strategies should be expanded. Specifically, new strategies should be developed that continue contact with stop-outs during their periods of nonattendance to reinforce their commitment to return.

It is common practice to continue retention efforts with continuing students who are considered "at risk" of dropping out. However, since stop-outs are already regarded as dropouts under the standard definition of continuing student, they are typically not exposed to retention efforts during their periods of nonattendance. Under our broader definition of continuing students, stop-outs should be regarded as retention successes in evaluations of conventional retention efforts, but their vulnerability to becoming dropouts and their candidacy for continued intervention during their periods of nonattendance should also be recognized.

During the planned stop-out period, inertia works against the student's actual return. The feelings of integration with college are likely to decline, and the influences of factors that compete with college attendance move to the forefront. This inertia should be countered with retention and marketing strategies that reinforce the nonattending students' continued "connectedness" to college and their educational goals and that convey the college's sincere interest in seeing that they achieve those goals.

Empirical evidence of the "at-risk" nature of the stop-out is provided by Saint Louis Community College survey data indicating that about 31 percent of fall nongraduates who did not return for the spring semester planned to return in the following fall, whereas examinations of actual returns revealed that only 16–17 percent actually re-enrolled the next fall. This difference might be attributed in part to some inherent bias in self-reported information, but we believe that the data reflect deviations from actual initial intent.

Although, as described above, the more appropriate accounting of retained students in evaluations of conventional retention efforts is important, the need to expand retention efforts to periods of nonattendance may be the more significant implication of our broader definition of continuing student. Whether the results of conventional efforts are good or bad, they may very well be near their maximum impact. Doing all that we can while a student is enrolled may not be enough if we lose contact with the student during periods of nonattendance.

New interventions directed to the nonattending student should, of course, be accompanied by evaluations of their impact. The remainder of the chapter focuses on the evaluation of a relatively simple and low-cost intervention presently being evaluated at Saint Louis Community College.

Evaluation of Intervention During a Period of Nonattendance

The evaluation discussed here examines an intervention at Saint Louis Community College designed to encourage the re-enrollment of fall semester students who did not graduate and did not return in the following spring semester. The intervention was implemented in summer 1990 for fall 1989 students who did not re-enroll for the spring 1990 semester. The evaluation examines the impact on fall 1990 return rates.

The specific activity evaluated was a direct mail contact in the form of two letters signed by the chancellor. The first letter, mailed in mid-July 1990, indicated that the student had been missed during the spring semester and expressed the college's continuing interest in helping the student achieve educational goals. The second letter, mailed two weeks later, asked the student to re-enroll and reminded him or her that registration was then taking place at all college locations.

Saint Louis Community College routinely determines the number of nonreturning nongraduates for consecutive semesters through a computer match of the graduate file and currently active student files for the two semesters. For the purposes of the evaluation, data for fall 1989 students who did not graduate and were not currently active in spring 1990 were extracted and saved as a separate file. These students were divided into an intervention group and a control group by means of a random-sample procedure. A 20 percent random sample ($N = 2,402$) received the intervention letters, while the remaining 80 percent ($N = 9,601$) served as the control group.

A variable designating each student in the extracted file as a member of either the intervention or control group was added to the other student characteristic data when the random sample was drawn. At the end of the late registration cycle for fall 1990, the extracted file was matched with the fall 1990 student file. Based on that matching a second variable was added, indicating the fall 1990 enrollment status (enrolled or not enrolled) for each student in the extracted file. The file was then ready for analysis.

The evaluation compares the respective return rates of the intervention and control groups, both in the aggregate and within student characteristic subsets. Thus far, the statistical significance of differences has been examined in terms of the chi-square for cross-tabulations of the intervention versus control group variable and the enrolled versus nonenrolled variable. Moreover, discriminant analysis has been used to assess whether information in the institutional data base can predict the "return potential" of students in the absence of any intervention. The development of a successful predictive equation will permit further evaluation of the relative impact of the intervention on students with "low return potential" and on those with "high return potential." More detailed evaluations are continuing; the initial findings are summarized below.

Aggregate Findings. The proportion of the control group who enrolled for the fall 1990 semester was 16.9 percent. This was consistent with previous years when the subsequent fall return rates of spring nonreturners were typically between 16 percent and 17 percent. The return rate for the intervention group was 18.6 percent. The difference in the control and intervention group rates is statistically significant at the $p < .05$ level.

Subset Findings. The most interesting subset findings were discovered when race and gender were controlled simultaneously. The apparent impact of the intervention was not statistically significant for either black females or white males. The impact on white females, a 19.3 percent return rate for the intervention group compared to a 16.8 percent rate for the control group, was significant at the $p < .05$ level. The greatest apparent impact in terms of both size and statistical significance was on black males. Only 14 percent of the control group returned, whereas 22.4 percent of the intervention group returned. The significance level was $p < .01$.

Discriminant Analysis of Return Potential. The impact of this or any other marketing activity that encourages former students to return is likely to be affected by what might be labeled the innate "return potential" of the individual students. The ability to accurately categorize students by return potential would be highly desirable for both the development and evaluation of marketing strategies.

This initial evaluation sought to categorize students as "high return potential" or "low return potential" students on the basis of a discriminant analysis within the control group. The discriminant grouping variable was the actual return or nonreturn for the fall 1990 semester. A variety of demographic and academic background variables available in the institutional student data base were included as discriminating variables. None of the equations derived in this analysis had sufficient discriminating power to provide a meaningful classification of students in terms of return potential.

Next Steps

One of the shortcomings of this initial evaluation is that it included all nonreturning nongraduates, that is, nondegree goal achievers and dropouts, as well as stop-outs, without distinguishing between them. This mix was unavoidable because distinguishing information is not available in the institutional data base, and we have not included student identifiers on nonreturning student surveys.

From a strict marketing point of view, the inclusion of nondegree goal achievers and dropouts in the mailing is probably desirable. Most businesses can attest that satisfied customers are one of the most fertile markets. In an era where a rapidly changing society and economy are making lifelong learning a necessity, a community college should certainly include goal achievers in its marketing strategy. Dropouts, that is, those students who do not re-enroll, do not achieve their goals, and have no intention of re-enrolling, are probably a less promising market. Their reasons for not returning, however, entail the same sort of external demands that cause other students to merely stop-out. Many dropouts also express a continued interest in their goals. With some encouragement, some of them may be able to move from dropping out to dealing with external demands through intermittent attendance.

For evaluation purposes, however, it is highly desirable that information on goal achievement and intent to return be included in the data base. We suspect that intent to return will be a key variable for the discriminant analysis of return potential. The hypothesis that intent to return may be an important predictor in the equation for return potential is consistent with Bean's (1980, 1981) findings that intent to leave is an excellent predictor of attrition. We also suspect that the true magnitude of the intervention's impact on stop-out return rates is obscured when the stop-outs are not distinguished from the other two categories of nondegree goal achievers and dropouts.

Student identifiers will be included on the questionnaire for the next nonreturning student survey, so the data base for the next evaluation will include data on goal achievement and intent to return for those students who respond to the survey. This inclusion will also allow us to include survey data regarding reasons for not re-enrolling, another variable that may be important in determining return potential.

Future analyses will also be expanded to include evaluations of the long-term impact of the initial intervention, the impact of further intervention after a second semester of nonattendance, and the impact of later intervention. In each instance, the same basic methodology of intervention versus control groups used in the initial evaluation will be employed.

Conclusion

The current and proposed research discussed here focuses on retention-driven marketing aimed at nonreturning nongraduates. We believe that these individuals constitute an important market that is often neglected due, in part, to a view of retention that is too narrow to be appropriate in the community college context. This focus should not, however, obscure the other ramifications of the proposed broader definition of a continuing student. Evaluations of more traditional retention efforts and evaluations of student outcomes must also recognize nondegree goals as legitimate educational achievements, and intermittent, but persistent, attendance as a valid method of pursuing educational goals. To do otherwise is to discount the educational pursuits and achievements of much of the adult population.

References

Bean, J. P. "Dropouts and Turnover: The Synthesis and Test of a Causal Model of Student Attrition." *Research in Higher Education,* 1980, *12,* 155–187.

Bean, J. P. "Student Attrition, Intentions, and Confidence: Interaction Effects in a Path Model (R^2 = .51)." Paper presented at the annual meeting of the American Research Association, Los Angeles, April 1981.

Pascarella, E. T., Duby, P. B., and Iverson, B. K. "A Test and Reconceptualization of a Theoretical Model of College Withdrawal in a Commuter Institution Setting." *Sociology of Education*, 1983, 52, 90–100.

Tinto, V. "Dropout from Higher Education: A Theoretical Synthesis of Recent Research." *Review of Educational Research*, 1975, 45, 89–125.

Tinto, V. *Leaving College: Rethinking the Causes and Cures of Student Attrition*. Chicago: University of Chicago Press, 1987.

Richard Tichenor is management information analyst at Saint Louis Community College, Saint Louis, Missouri. His areas of expertise include survey research and program evaluation.

John J. Cosgrove is director of institutional research and planning at Saint Louis Community College. His areas of expertise include policy analysis and assessment of institutional effectiveness.

Modern marketing, financial aid, and retention strategies require an ongoing process of strategic decision making and evaluation in order to ensure their effectiveness.

Monitoring Shifts in Campus Image and Recruitment Efforts in Small Colleges

David Murray

Evaluation of recruitment and retention programs is frequently a combination of intuition and science at small colleges. Like colleges and universities everywhere, small colleges have a need for evaluation. Unlike the evaluation efforts typically found at large public and private colleges, however, most small colleges do not have large institutional research offices. In many instances, small institutions cannot afford a formal institutional research office. Under these circumstances, institutional research and evaluation studies must be squeezed into the busy schedules of campus administrators who have other full-time responsibilities. Occasionally, faculty members are released from teaching or hired during the summer to perform institutional studies.

Lolli (this volume) notes that campus trend data and comparative information from similar institutions can be useful for evaluating recruitment and retention programs. Small colleges often rely heavily on trend data and comparative information because they may lack the time and resources to conduct more sophisticated evaluation studies.

This chapter describes parts of the ongoing evaluation of recruitment and retention activities at DePauw University. DePauw does not have a large institutional research office. There is a Bureau of Testing, which focuses on research and support for the academic program, leaving most administrative departments to conduct their own research. Despite the lack of an institutional research office, research is especially important at DePauw these days. Beyond the normal exigencies in the life of a college, exacerbated by the decline in the number of high school graduates, DePauw has been changing. In order to monitor the effects of these changes on recruitment and retention efforts, ongoing evaluation is needed.

NEW DIRECTIONS FOR INSTITUTIONAL RESEARCH, no. 70, Summer 1991 © Jossey-Bass Inc., Publishers

Without an institutional research office to look at recruitment and retention programs, DePauw relies heavily on institutional trend data and comparative information to assess the effectiveness of its recruitment and retention activities. This chapter provides a brief description of DePauw, followed by discussion of three recruitment and retention initiatives. These initiatives include the recruitment of large numbers of minority students, the strategic use of financial aid, and the use of a new market-segmentation system. The evaluation of these activities is less formal than might be found at larger institutions, but it is no less important to the long-term vitality of this small institution. In order to illustrate how internal trend data and comparative information are used to assess the effectiveness of each of these initiatives, details on each of these activities are provided in addition to a discussion of evaluation efforts.

Founded in 1837, DePauw University is a selective, entirely undergraduate university. DePauw's twenty-three hundred students, who come from forty-four states and thirty-one countries, are enrolled in its Asbury College of Liberal Arts (twenty-three departments with over thirty majors), School of Music, and School of Nursing. Located forty miles west of Indianapolis in Greencastle, Indiana, the university has an endowment of over $130 million. Over the past decade, DePauw has added new programs and facilities. The quality of the student body improved noticeably as the applicant pool increased significantly. These developments were the result of institutional planning, recruitment, and retention strategies.

Increasing Ethnic Diversity

In summer 1986, DePauw inaugurated its eighteenth president, who clearly articulated priorities for improving the academic and cocurricular life of the campus, including a plan to dramatically increase the presence of ethnic minorities in the student body, faculty, and staff and curriculum. The black community was targeted first because DePauw had better alumni ties to the black community than to any other nonwhite segment of our society and because DePauw was especially concerned about the declining college-bound rate in an expanding black population and the resultant economic, political, and social implications of this decline for the United States.

The number of black students has steadily increased. In 1986 black students comprised 1 percent of the entering freshman class. By fall 1990 black students made up 10 percent of the entering class. The number of black faculty and staff has also increased from two to twelve during the same time period. In addition, faculty interested in serving as advisers for ethnic minority students were also sought. Black men and women who have made outstanding contributions to a wide range of fields and walks of life have routinely become a part of the university lecture, arts, convocation, and symposium programs. Financial aid efforts targeted at black students and their families were also expanded.

A trend analysis of the enrollment rates of black students indicates that recruitment efforts have succeeded. In the four-year period 1986–1990, black student enrollments increased 1,000 percent. In order to evaluate the effectiveness of DePauw's efforts to increase black student enrollments, it is also important to compare the retention rates of these students. Table 1 indicates that retention rates for black students compare favorably with those of other minority students at DePauw.

Comparative data for similar schools can be difficult to secure, but Porter (1989), in a study conducted for the National Institute of Independent Colleges and Universities, found that from 1980–1986 the mean six-year graduation rate for black students at public colleges and universities was 28 percent, compared to 31 percent at independent colleges and universities. The four-year graduation rate of nearly 65 percent at DePauw looks healthy by comparison. While there is a simple, standard statistical test of the differences between two proportions, it was not applied to these data because of the magnitude of the differences. The differences were judged to be substantively significant. Of course, background characteristics and other factors may differ among black students at DePauw, but internal trend data and comparative figures from independent colleges and universities suggest that DePauw has been successful at retaining black students.

Evaluating Financial Aid Trends

Like many private schools, DePauw continually evaluates the impact of financial aid need and awards upon new-student matriculation. Analyses of trend data have revealed that financial need and the impact of aid awards differ by family characteristics. Figure 1 presents data for ethnic minority students enrolled at DePauw among all four years of study. The

Table 1. Three-Year Averages of Students Returning for the Second Year and Graduation Rates by Race

Race	Returned Second Year, Entered 1987–1989 (DePauw University)	Graduated in Four Years, Entered 1984–1986 (DePauw University)	Graduated in Six Years, 1980–1986 (All Private Colleges)
Black	83.3	64.7	31.0
Asian	81.5	66.7	58.0
Hispanic	68.8	50.0	25.0
All Students	90.0	71.6	54.0

Note: Figures are percentages.

Sources: DePauw University Office of the Registrar, 1990; Porter, 1989.

Figure 1. Fall 1990 Average Financial Need (All Current Students)

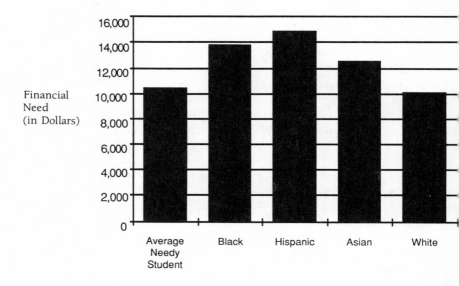

Source: DePauw University Office of Financial Aid, 1990.

average need among black and Hispanic students is noticeably higher than it is for majority students. In order to increase the enrollment of minority students, the university has had to increase the amount of financial aid awarded to black and Hispanic students.

The financial aid office has also noted a decline in the number of students filing the financial aid form (FAF) in recent years. Over the three-year period of fall 1988 to fall 1990, the number of students filing FAFs has dropped by almost 50 percent. Institutional trend data reveal a decline in the number of middle-income families applying for financial aid. Not only are they applying in smaller numbers, but when they do apply and are accepted, relatively few enroll.

Table 2 provides information about DePauw's yield rate, that is, the percentage of accepted students who actually enroll, among families with varying combinations of income and FAF-computed need. It is the middle-income group about which campus administrators are most concerned. Of particular concern is the group of students from families with adjusted gross incomes between $40,000 and $80,000 whose financial needs range between $2,500 and $8,499 per year. For students entering in fall 1990, the amount of scholarship in a student's financial aid package (a combination of scholarships, loans, and jobs) was substantially increased. Even so, the resulting effect on yield was minimal.

Table 2. 1988 Parental IRS-Adjusted Gross Income
and Fall 1989 Financial Aid Need Among Applicants

FAF Need / Parental Income	< $10,000	≥ $10,000 ≤ $40,000	≥ $40,001 ≤ $80,000	≥ $80,001	Total
≥ $8,500	20/30 = 67%	116/202 = 57%	41/101 = 41%	1/1 = 100%	178/334 = 53%
≤ $8,499 ← ≥ $2,500	0/2 = 0%	12/28 = 43%	31/137 = 23%	0/7 = 0%	43/174 = 25%
≤ $2,499 ← 0	3/56 = 5%	6/17 = 35%	57/166 = 34%	51/110 = 46%	117/349 = 34%
Total	23/88 = 26%	134/247 = 54%	129/404 = 32%	52/118 = 44%	338/857 = 39%

Note: Figures are ratios, also expressed as percentages, of accepted students who actually enrolled to the total number of accepted students. Financial aid need was computed on the basis of information provided by each family on the financial aid form (FAF).

Source: DePauw University Office of Financial Aid, 1990.

The second group of concern is students with zero demonstrated financial need, that is, need in the range of $1 to $2,499. These families would be classified in national statistics as middle-income students and families. But the first group identified above represents students and families that the admissions and financial aid offices have classified as the "DePauw" middle-income group. This discrepancy in who qualifies as a middle-income family is not owing to the nature of DePauw's financial aid packages. The problem is the federally mandated congressional methodology (CM) that is the basis for analysis of the family's FAF. This methodology does not always discriminate effectively when it comes to identifying middle-income families. For example, CM essentially assumes that the cost of living is the same in Greencastle, Indiana, as it is in Chicago, Los Angeles, or Honolulu. The difference in housing costs and other consumer items, however, can vary widely across these locales.

Another problem concerns home equity. Currently CM expects the family to have access to a certain percentage of home equity as an asset toward the cost of a college education. One can argue at length about the merits and demerits of tapping home equity, but there are some students and families who cannot use their home equity. For instance, if a family lives in an area where the cost of housing has been appreciating dramatically, considerable home equity may have been created. However, if the family's income has not increased proportionately, that family is not able to afford the interest payments on a second mortgage or home equity loan.

To get better information from students and families, information that is not required for the FAF, DePauw's financial aid staff has developed a special form that goes immediately to any student applying for admission who indicates that he or she will be a candidate for financial aid. The form asks for additional, quantifiable information, but it also asks for attitudinal information, such as what the family realistically thinks it will be able to contribute to the student's education. Sometimes the family's estimate has no basis in financial reality, and thus there is probably nothing DePauw can do for the student or family involved. For many families, however, the assessments are realistic and come close to estimating what the families fairly can do to support the students' educations once we have a true reading on their ability to pay. In either case, early in the process the financial aid staff has new information with which to work and, perhaps, an early warning about those families with potential FAF analysis problems.

In a major step, DePauw has committed funds to middle-income families with objective needs for additional assistance. In turn, admissions and financial aid staff are able to talk about this commitment in all of their personal contacts with students, families, and high school college counselors. Staff in both offices spend additional time with students and families. To the extent permitted within the "professional judgment" limitations of the federal law establishing CM, financial aid counselors have been responsive to the unique situations of many middle-income families.

Yield rates among various income groups continue to be evaluated in order to determine whether increased aid has an impact on the matriculation rates of middle-income students. In addition, an evaluation of the increased personal assistance provided by the financial aid office has been conducted. High school counselors and student prospects have been surveyed. The results indicate that both high school counselors and student prospects identify DePauw as a college that is willing to help middle-income families. However, an important problem remains. Many students make cost decisions before they ever apply, dismissing colleges for cost reasons based on the list prices of the education. These prejudgments are especially prevalent in relation to private colleges like DePauw.

To combat this situation and the demographic trends, colleges buy the names of an increasing number of prospective students through programs like the College Board's Student Search Service and the American College Testing Program's Equal Opportunity Service. Colleges engage in this practice with the hope that if they correspond with a large number of prospects, more students will apply and, if accepted, enroll. However, some students may have already written off a particular college (or type of college) as ill-matched to their needs. DePauw's data suggest that this is increasingly true for those who will need financial aid to attend a college or university, among them a growing number of students from middle-income families.

Unless a student applies for admission and financial aid, DePauw may never have a chance to talk about possible assistance. The challenge, therefore, is to identify students and families who may have cost concerns *before* the students decide where they will apply. To meet this challenge, colleges must devise methods to target students at an early juncture, the preapplication stage, when the institutions frequently have little more than students' mailing addresses. The admissions office at DePauw is currently exploring a market segmentation system that *may* help.

PRIZM

In 1974 Claritas, a firm based in New York City, developed a new market-segmentation system called PRIZM. The basic assumption of the PRIZM approach is that people who cluster in neighborhoods tend to come from similar income ranges and have similar educational backgrounds. They also tend to value the same things, from the cars they drive to their favorite music, to their predispositions (or lack thereof) to things and activities such as passports, bowling, and contributions to public television.

In developing PRIZM, Claritas initially used 1970 census data. Socioeconomic and general demographic data, all public information, were organized, and a mathematical modeling technique was applied to form cluster groups. An optimum number of clusters was sought, that is, the number and types of clusters that would maximize the homogeneity within a cluster and simultaneously maximize the differences between cluster groups.

Optimally, forty cluster groups were identified, then they were organized into a dozen social group codes that brought together somewhat similar cluster types. The PRIZM clusters and their eye-catching labels are listed in Table 3. To give some feel for the descriptions of these clusters, here is what Claritas has to say in brief about Blue Blood Estates and Shotguns & Pickups (College Information Systems, 1989, pp. 174, 179):

> *Blue Blood Estates*—America's wealthiest socioeconomic neighborhoods, populated by super-upper established managers, professionals, and heirs to "old money," accustomed to privilege and living in luxurious surroundings. One in ten millionaires can be found in Blue Blood Estates, and there is a considerable drop from these heights to the next level of affluence.

> *Shotguns & Pickups*—Shotguns & Pickups aggregates hundreds of small, outlying townships and crossroad villages that serve the nation's breadbasket and other rural areas. They lead the nation in mobile homes and show peak indices for large families with school-age children, headed by blue-collar craftsmen, equipment operators, and transport workers with high school educations. These areas are home to many dedicated outdoorsmen.

The DePauw admissions office has started to use PRIZM in several ways. College Information Systems (CIS), the Chicago-based firm that has developed unique targeting applications of the PRIZM system for the college market, has analyzed DePauw's mailing list of inquiries, its applicant pool, and its currently enrolled student body to determine the predominant cluster types at each of these stages. The results are interesting. For example, certain PRIZM cluster types are very prevalent in the applicant pool, but, once admitted, students from some of these clusters will turn over in very large percentages into enrolling students whereas the yield rates for other groups will remain relatively anemic.

One application of the PRIZM cluster groupings that CIS developed specifically for DePauw has been to screen our College Board Student Search names, which the college purchases each year. In 1990 the admissions office purchased more names than it intended to use and then reduced the number of names to whom it sent direct mailings. DePauw actually trimmed names that the PRIZM analysis suggested would be least productive. Presumably, the names that were used will lead to better response rates and additional applications than would have been the case without PRIZM screening.

Table 3. PRIZM System Life-Style Clusters (Block-Group Model)

Group Codes	Numbers	Nicknames	Percentage of 1987 U.S. Households
S1	28	Blue Blood Estates	1.13
	8	Money & Brains	0.94
	5	Furs & Station Wagons	3.19
S2	7	Pools & Patios	3.42
	25	Two More Rungs	0.74
	20	Young Influentials	2.86
S3	24	Young Suburbia	5.40
	30	Blue-Chip Blues	6.04
U1	21	Urban Gold Coast	0.48
	37	Bohemian Mix	1.14
	31	Black Enterprise	0.76
	23	New Beginnings	4.32
T1	1	God's Country	2.71
	17	New Homesteaders	4.16
	12	Towns & Gowns	1.15
S4	27	Levittown, U.S.A.	3.05
	39	Gray Power	2.94
	2	Rank & File	1.41
T2	40	Blue-Collar Nursery	2.24
	16	Middle America	3.19
	29	Coalburg & Corntown	1.93
U2	3	New Melting Pot	0.90
	36	Old Yankee Rows	1.59
	14	Emergent Minorities	1.72
	26	Single City Blues	3.35
R1	19	Shotguns & Pickups	1.85
	34	Agri-Business	2.09
	35	Grain Belt	1.24
T3	33	Golden Ponds	5.25
	22	Mines & Mills	2.84
	13	Norma Rae-Ville	2.34
	18	Smalltown Downtown	2.44
R2	10	Back-Country Folks	3.43
	38	Share Croppers	3.98
	15	Tobacco Roads	1.22
	6	Hard Scrabble	1.50
U3	4	Heavy Industry	2.73
	11	Downtown Dixie-Style	3.37
	9	Hispanic Mix	1.88
	32	Public Assistance	3.10
		TOTAL U.S.	**100.0**

te: These are the forty PRIZM life-style clusters, organized into twelve broad social groups. The groups are
led "S" for suburban, "U" for urban, "T" for towns, and "R" for rural and are shown from top to bottom in
scending socioeconomic rank, with the group numbers (S1, S2, S3, and so on) indicating these ranks.
e Numbers column represents the cluster number assigned to the individual PRIZM cluster.

rce: College Information Systems, 1989, p. 47.

To evaluate the success of this strategy, a control group of students was created. A sample of College Board Student Search names, including names that would have been eliminated by the PRIZM methodology, were sent all of the standard mailings from the university. The preliminary results from a comparison of experimental and control groups indicate that the students rated highly by the PRIZM system have applied for fall 1991 in noticeably higher percentages than the students targeted by PRIZM to be eliminated from DePauw's direct mail list.

The admissions staff is also trying to use PRIZM to target the DePauw "middle-income student." PRIZM has the potential to tell admissions offices much about a family's socioeconomic and demographic background simply by the street address. PRIZM's goal is to refine the analytic system to the level of a single city block, thus differentiating one neighborhood block from the next. DePauw's goal is to be able to identify students and neighborhoods so precisely that there is a high probability that a given neighborhood and its predominant cluster type are homogeneous. If that level of precision is possible, then the admissions staff can identify certain cluster types that exhibit certain kinds of financial aid characteristics (for example, students with high need, students from DePauw's "middle-income" families, students with the ability to pay most or all of the costs of a DePauw education). Such precise identification would enable the college to target very specific messages to these groups. Similar approaches may make it possible to target black and other ethnic minority students more effectively. The PRIZM system may have the potential to identify those students with the greatest likelihood of matriculation.

Consider Table 4 and the target groups developed for DePauw by CIS. By breaking down the PRIZM cluster groups in this fashion, the admissions staff are able to evaluate the effects of targeting mailings and to identify student/family clusters that have the highest yield rates for DePauw.

There are two cluster groups that have financial aid application rates of 40 percent or higher. Since roughly 35 percent of all DePauw applicants apply for financial aid, clearly these two groups exceed the cluster-group-average application rates. However, no cluster group exceeds a 55 percent financial aid application rate, which means at least 45 percent of the families in these groups are not applying for financial aid. This situation results in inefficient use of staff time and institutional funds. Over time, the admissions staff hopes to identify the PRIZM groups that are most responsive to DePauw mailings and to determine the marketing activities that are most attractive to students and families.

Remembering that each cluster group is composed of individual clusters, the admissions staff is working with CIS to further refine their analyses. Within some of these clustered social groups there are individual clusters showing financial aid application rates well beyond 55 percent. For example, we have identified one cluster type composed primarily of middle-income families that has a 70 percent financial aid application rate.

Table 4. Financial Aid Applicants by DePauw PRIZM Target Groups

Target Groups	Total Admissions Applicants	Total Aid Applicants	Percentage of Admissions Applicants
Affluent suburban families (Clusters 28, 8, 5)	1,238	217	18
Young town/suburban families (Clusters 20, 24, 1, 12)	1,014	333	33
Older neighborhoods (Clusters 7, 25)	415	106	26
Mid-scale blue-collar families (Clusters 40, 16, 29)	693	378	55
All other neighborhoods (All other clusters)	1,439	626	44
Totals	4,799	1,660	35

Source: College Information Systems, 1989, p. 146.

We are also looking at specific geographical breakdowns. When combined with individual or group-cluster types, this geographical analysis may help identify neighborhoods where there is even a greater homogeneity than we can presently detect, neighborhoods where there will be largely uniform reactions to some of the "messages" DePauw may send. The CIS staff also has indicated that the admissions staff can take PRIZM data one more step by passing them through other commercially available mailing-list systems that further refine target populations.

At DePauw, we are just beginning the process of evaluating whether or not PRIZM can be applied in the marketing of colleges. The system has been used for several years now by many top corporations to target their sales of a wide range of products, but it remains to be seen whether the system can be used to better target the marketing of DePauw University. If we can refine its use to the point that it can, with a high degree of probability, target certain market groups (for example, DePauw middle-income families), it may represent a real breakthrough. Only further evaluation of PRIZM will demonstrate its effectiveness. We will need to determine not only whether PRIZM enables DePauw to more effectively target student prospects at an earlier stage in the admissions process but also whether a cost-benefit analysis is required.

Conclusion

Evaluation of the impact of recruitment and retention activities is difficult. Federal, state, and institutional financial aid policies change each year. New buildings, new faculty, and new students also mean that college campuses are always constantly recreating themselves. The task of tracking the impact of recruitment and retention activities requires campus administrators to study a constantly moving target. Although many small colleges lack the resources to conduct systematic program evaluations, DePauw is committed to using comparative and institutional trend data, along with occasional formal evaluation studies, and strategic thinking to monitor its recruitment and retention activities.

References

College Information Systems. *Institutional Research Report*. Northfield, Ill.: Claritas Corporation, 1989.
Porter, O. *Undergraduate Completion and Persistence at Four-Year Colleges and Universities: Completers, Persisters, Stopouts, and Dropouts*. Washington, D.C.: National Institute of Independent Colleges and Universities, 1989.

David Murray is director of admissions and assistant vice-president at DePauw University, Greencastle, Indiana, and oversees the admissions and financial aid programs. He has worked in business systems for Eastman Kodak and previously held positions in admissions, financial aid, and student affairs at Saint Lawrence University, Canton, New York, and Syracuse University, Syracuse, New York.

Evaluation of recruitment and retention programs requires an ongoing commitment to evaluation and a willingness to look at academic policies and procedures.

Evaluating Recruitment and Retention Programs

Don Hossler

Evaluation of recruitment and retention programs is complex. No single template can be developed that will fit the evaluation needs of all institutions. Chapters Three through Seven illustrate a diverse set of evaluation activities and how they have been approached by a large public university, two large private universities, a public two-year college, and a small private liberal arts college. The approaches reflect the unique problems faced by different sectors of the American higher education system.

As both the proportion of students enrolling in private institutions and the number of traditional age students have declined, the private sector has become increasingly dependent on sophisticated marketing strategies and the use of financial aid to help recruit and retain students. These strategies have become necessary to maintain the health and vitality of many private colleges and universities. These strategies, however, are expensive. Frances (1990) estimates that among private institutions, the institutionally funded student aid portion of tuition revenues has increased from approximately 19 percent in 1975–1976 to more than 25 percent in 1985–1986. Estimates of the cost of recruiting students are difficult to obtain. The true cost of recruitment may be spread across budgets in the publications office, admissions, institutional advancement, and the president's office, among others. Werth (1988) calculated that some Ivy League institutions may spend as much as $1,300 per matriculated student. The point is that financial aid and student recruitment have become expensive propositions at private colleges and universities. It is no accident that three

The author thanks Michael Dolence for his contributions to this chapter.

chapters on evaluation at private institutions, those by Pagano and Terkla (Chapter Three) at Tufts University, Wilcox (Chapter Four) at Rensselaer Polytechnic Institute, and Murray (Chapter Seven) at DePauw University, focused on the evaluation of recruitment activities and the impact of student financial aid on student matriculation and retention. In light of the cost of these activities, campus administrators can ill afford to ignore questions about the effectiveness of these programs.

Public institutions, both two- and four-year, face a different set of problems. Although the recruitment practices of public colleges and universities have become more aggressive, these institutions still enjoy a large competitive advantage because of their low costs. As a result, public colleges and universities are not as concerned about the recruitment of new students. For a variety of reasons, however, they are concerned about student retention. In many states, higher education coordinating boards or state legislatures have made public institutions more accountable for their activities. Student retention rates are often used as one measure of institutional effectiveness. In the case of public community colleges, student attrition is a major concern. The American College Testing Program (1989) estimates that nearly 50 percent of all entering students fail to re-enroll for their sophomore year. For public community colleges, an increase in the number of students retained can have a dramatic impact on student enrollments.

The unique characteristics of most small colleges also merit discussion. Institutional research looks very different at many small colleges. In theory, good evaluation practices should be generalizable to all colleges and universities. In practice, few small colleges can afford to maintain a full-time institutional research office to conduct the kinds of evaluation studies described here in Chapters Three through Six. At many small institutions, evaluation is an ad hoc activity. Murray's description of evaluation activities at DePauw University is a realistic look at how the offices of admissions and financial aid at DePauw use trend data and comparative information from other institutions to make judgments about the effectiveness of their recruitment and retention efforts. Other small institutions with limited resources could undoubtedly benefit from the methods of some of the more thorough evaluations described in this volume. Improved evaluation procedures could lead to more effective use of limited resources. Even without a formal institutional research office, thoughtful administrators seek as much evaluative information as possible to help them make decisions about program effectiveness.

Limits to Evaluation

Evaluation can provide useful information about the effectiveness of recruitment and retention programs. As with any evaluation activities, however, there are limitations to what can be learned.

Recruitment and Retention Programs Are Moving Targets. The college choice process is a longitudinal endeavor that is influenced primarily by a complex web of family background factors and, to a lesser extent, by institutional recruitment practices (Hossler, Braxton, and Coopersmith, 1989). Similarly, students' decisions to withdraw are complex and do not lend themselves easily to intervention activities (Bean, 1990). New-student enrollments at Whatsamatta U. may have increased by 10 percent after a year in which financial aid awards to new students increased by 20 percent, the admissions office inaugurated a new recruitment strategy, the basketball team made it to the semifinals of the National Collegiate Athletic Association Tournament, four new academic programs were initiated, and the student union was refurbished. Whatsamatta U. may also have started an advising program for undecided majors that same year, and the number of freshmen who returned for their sophomore year may have increased by 6 percent. But just as institutional researchers must be careful in the design of evaluation activities, so too they must be cautious in their interpretation of the results. Attribution of increases or decreases in student enrollments to any single activity is difficult. Repeated evaluations of programs and examinations of patterns over time may be necessary to determine the effectiveness of recruitment and retention programs.

Repeated evaluations are a good idea. Just as researchers look for results that can be replicated to validate theories, institutional researchers should routinely repeat evaluative studies every two or three years. Although the effects of financial aid strategies or the impact of a retention intervention should not be expected to change each year, they may change over time. New financial aid programs emanating from federal, state, or competing institutions may alter the perceived value of an institution's financial aid programs. Admission standards or the level of rigor in a popular academic major may have an impact on student persistence rates. As Murray (Chapter Seven) observes, evaluation of the effects of recruitment and retention programs involves the study of targets that are constantly in flux. What appeared to be an accurate depiction of the effects of a recruitment program in 1990 may not be accurate in 1993. Efforts to monitor the effectiveness of recruitment and retention programs must be continuous.

Evaluation Is a Political Process. There are several prerequisites for effective evaluations of recruitment and retention programs. For every evaluation, institutional researchers and administrative decision makers who will utilize the evaluation results must clearly identify its purposes and goals. Unfortunately, institutional researchers often find themselves caught between what they thought were the goals of the evaluation and what turn out to be the real goals. As Dolence (this volume) points out, evaluations often have political dimensions that should not be overlooked. Institutional researchers must attend to the political environment in which they work. Efforts to clearly outline the scope and intent of program evaluations can save time and misunderstandings at the end of the process. Sound evaluation of recruitment and retention programs is essential, but the programs cannot be isolated from issues of curriculum, quality of instruction, graduation requirements, and other academic concerns.

Placing Evaluation Within the Big Picture

This volume focuses on the evaluation of specific recruitment and retention activities. It would be a mistake, however, for campus administrators to focus exclusively on specific programmatic interventions such as a new mailing strategy to increase new-student enrollments or a new advising system to increase student retention. These programmatic interventions can influence recruitment and retention, but there are underlying issues related to the strength and vitality of academic programs and institutional images that have a more powerful impact on recruitment and retention. In addition, academic policies and procedures can also affect student recruitment and retention.

Academic Programs. Student college choice research has consistently demonstrated that perceived academic quality is frequently the most important reason that students offer for selecting one college or university over another (Hossler, Braxton, and Coopersmith, 1989). At small colleges the overall image of the institution may be more important than the image of any single program; however, at larger universities students may enroll on the basis of the strength and reputation of a specific major or academic program. Similarly, as Howard and Rogers (this volume) note, retention rates can vary across departments or schools.

The importance of academic programs cannot be overlooked. Analyses of long-term enrollment and persistence rates across departments should be conducted on a regular basis. Trend data may point to concerns that require further study. A high dropout rate may be a function of appropriate academic rigor, or it may be the result of poor teaching and faculty who are never available to students. Low new-student enrollments may be the result of low student demand for a particular major, or it may be the result of a weak reputation and faculty who never follow up with prospective students.

Although the politics of evaluating academic programs can be daunting, evaluators should periodically assess the impact of academic programs on recruitment and retention. Once data are collected, evaluators should work closely with departmental and other academic administrators to devise the most effective methods for circulating the information. If care is not exercised, faculty are likely to become defensive and nonresponsive to the data.

Policies and Procedures. In addition to academic programs, academic policies and procedures should be periodically evaluated. Lolli (this volume) notes the potential impact of the speed of transfer credit evaluations on potential transfers. Similarly, Howard and Rogers (this volume) discuss the potential impact of changes in graduation requirements on persistence rates. The evaluation of recruitment and retention programs goes beyond individual programs. Campus administrators should recognize that programs, policies, and procedures comprise a system. Changes in the system, or changes in attitudes of students toward elements of the system, can have an effect on student recruitment and persistence.

Innovative recruitment and retention programs are not a panacea for all institutional enrollment concerns. The academic programs, institutional image, and campus environment exert the strongest influence on the enrollment and persistence decisions of students. Nevertheless, effective recruitment programs can influence students' decisions when they are choosing between two similar institutions. Similarly, retention initiatives can influence students' decisions to persist. Recruitment and retention programs, however, can require significant investments of staff time and institutional dollars. Many colleges and universities are spending scarce resources on recruitment and retention programs. These programs should be integrated into the strategic planning process of each campus, and they should be viewed within the larger context of academic programs, policies, and administrative systems. In order to be confident that institutional resources are spent wisely, ongoing evaluations of these programs, policies, and administrative systems should be routinely conducted.

References

American College Testing Program. *National Dropout Rates: Compiled for the ACT National Center for the Advancement of Educational Practices.* Ames, Iowa: American College Testing Program, 1989.

Bean, J. P. "Why Students Leave: Insights from Research." In D. Hossler, J. P. Bean, and Associates (eds.), *The Strategic Management of College Enrollments.* San Francisco: Jossey-Bass, 1990.

Frances, C. *What Factors Affect College Tuition? A Guide to the Facts and Issues.* Washington, D.C.: Association of State Colleges and Universities, 1990.

Hossler, D., Braxton, J., and Coopersmith, G. "Understanding Student College Choice." In J. C. Smart (ed.), *Higher Education: Handbook of Theory and Research.* Vol. 5. New York: Agathon, 1989.

Werth, B. "Why Is College so Expensive? Maybe America Wants It That Way." *Change Magazine,* Mar.–Apr. 1988, pp. 13–25.

Don Hossler is associate professor and chair of the Department of Educational Leadership and Policy Studies in the School of Education, Indiana University, Bloomington.

INDEX

Academic policies/programs, as recruitment/retention factor, 98–99
Academic progress, tracking of, 61–72
Accepted-applicant surveys, 39, 41–43
Administration, and evaluation, 28–30; role of, 9–10
Admissions research, 33–45
American College Test (ACT) scores, analysis of, 15, 16, 66
American College Testing Program, 96, 99
Anderson, C. H., 50, 59
Asian students, return rates of, 85
Astin, A. W., 69, 72

Barberini, P. G., 47, 60
Beal, P. E., 17, 19
Bean, J. P., 30, 32, 80, 97, 99
Bennett, W., 47
Black students, 84–85; and financial aid, 85–86
Bradburn, N. M., 11, 19
Braxton, J., 97, 98, 99
Brinkman, P. T., 69, 72
Budget, for evaluation, 27–28

Campus visits, evaluation of, 40–41
Census data, 89–90
Chapman, D., 14, 18
Chapman, R. G., 49, 50, 56
Claritas, 89–90. See also PRIZM
Cluster groupings. See PRIZM
Cockriel, I. W., 50, 60
Cohorts, in student populations, 64–65
College Board, 15, 18, 47, 49, 59
College Information Systems (CIS), 90–93, 94
Community colleges, retention in, 73–81
Computing, and evaluation, 1–2, 28. See also Data bases, Information systems
Congressional methodology (CM), for evaluating financial need, 83–84
Contacts, institutional. See Institutional contacts
Continuing students, 76. See also Community colleges

Coopersmith, G., 97, 98, 99
Cosgrove, J. J., 2, 73–81
Cost-benefit perspective, 6
Costs, of college education, 47

Data bases, development and management of, 2, 62–68. See also Information systems, Longitudinal tracking system
Decentralization, of tracking systems, 62–64
Demographic variables, 66
DePauw University, evaluation at, 2, 83–94
Direct mail, evaluation of, 78
Discenza, R., 17, 19
Dolence, M. G., 1, 5–19, 21, 97
Dropouts, and return potential, 79–80
Duby, P. B., 74, 81

Ellickson, K., 50, 59
Endo, J. J., 22, 32
Enrollment Planning Service. See College Board
Enrollment, student, 1, 9–10; evaluation of, 2, 28–29. See also Recruitment, Retention
Ethnic diversity, 84–85
Evaluation, 1–3, 22–24; of academic progress, 61–72; benefits of, 25–26, 28–31; costs of, 95–96; and financial aid, 47–60, 85–89; framework for, 8–11; and information systems, 25–31; and institutional contacts, 33–45; intent of, 6; limits of, 96–98; of marketing, 73–81; questions for, 11–14; role of, 7–8, 11; scope of, 7; in small colleges, 83–94, 96; types of, 8. See also Enrollment, Personnel evaluation, Recruitment, Reporting, Research, Retention
Ewell, P. T., 62, 64, 72

Fenske, R. H., 59
Ferguson, J. M., 17, 19
Financial aid, 2, 3; 47–48; evaluation of, 48–60, 85–89, 92–93; purposes of, 48
Financial aid form (FAF), 86, 88

Four-year institutions, and retention, 73–74

Frances, C., 95, 99

Goal-attainment perspective, 6
Gowen, D. B., 5, 19
Graduation statistics, 68–69, 70–71
Grajeda, J., 9, 19
Green, T. F., 5, 19

Hardware. See Computing
Hardy, C., 9, 19
Hispanic students, 85; and financial aid, 85–86
Home equity, and financial aid, 88
Hossler, D., 1–3, 10, 15, 16, 19, 22, 32, 49, 59, 95–99
Howard, R. D., 2, 61–72, 98, 99
Huff, R. P., 48, 59

Iba, D. L., 50, 60
Information systems, student, 1–2, 10, 21–31; costs of, 29–30; development of, 26–27; resources for, 27–28. See also Data bases, Longitudinal tracking system, System design
Institution last attended (ILA), analysis of, 15–16
Institutional contacts, evaluation of, 33–45
Interpretation, role of, 23–24
Iverson, B. K., 74, 81

Jackson, G., 14, 19
Jackson, R., 49, 50, 56

Keller, G., 7, 19
Key performance indicators (KPIs), 16

Lay, R. S., 22, 32
Leadership. See Administration
Lenning, O. T., 17, 19
Life-style clusters, 91. See also PRIZM
LISREL (linear structural relationships), 52
Litten, L., 22, 32
Lolli, A., 1–2, 11, 21–32, 67, 83, 98–99
Longitudinal tracking system, 62–68; examples of, 69–72; statistics from, 68–69

McCreery, A., 7, 19
McLaughlin, G. W., 64, 72

McLaughlin, J. S., 64, 72
Maguire, J., 22, 32
Market classification system, 15
Marketing: retention-driven, 2, 73–81; segmentation system for, 89–93
Matrix, for evaluation, 11, 12–13; of financial aid, 54–58
Merit scholarships. See No-need scholarships
Middle-income families, and financial need, 88–89, 92
Miyahara, D., 9, 18
Moline, A. E., 52, 60
Murdock, T. A., 51, 60
Murray, D., 2, 83–94, 96, 97

National Association of Student Financial Aid Administrators, 49
National Collegiate Athletic Association (NCAA) classification, 35–36, 72
National Institute of Independent Colleges and Universities, 85
Neighborhoods, and market analysis. See PRIZM
Noblitt, M. T., 26, 32
No-need scholarships, 50–52, 56–57. See also Financial aid
Nora, A., 52, 60
North Carolina State University, 2
Nuetzel, J., 50, 59

Pagano, M. F., 2, 33–45, 96
Parents: evaluating impressions of, 43–44; income of, 87
Pascarella, E. T., 57, 60, 74, 81
Personnel evaluation, vs. program evaluation, 22–23
Politics, and evaluation, 6, 11, 27, 97–98
Popham, W. J., 23, 24, 32
Porter, J. D., 47, 60
Porter, O., 85, 94
Pratt, L. K., 70, 72
PRIZM, 89–93
Programs. See Academic, Recruitment, Retention
Public institutions, recruitment and retention at, 96. See also Recruitment, Retention

Rapp, C., 9, 18
Recruitment, evaluation of, 1 3, 14–16, 95–99; context for, 5–19; and financial aid,

49–51, 85–89, 92–93; at small colleges, 83–94. *See also* Enrollment, Evaluation, Retention

Rensselaer Polytechnic Institution, 2; and evaluation of financial aid, 48, 52–60

Reporting, *vs.* evaluation, 23–24

Research, *vs.* evaluation, 23–24

Reserve Officers' Training Corps (ROTC), as enrollment incentive, 55–56

Retention classification system, 17

Retention, evaluation of, 1–3, 16–17, 95–99; in community colleges, 73–81; context for, 5–19; and financial aid, 51–52, 57–58; at small colleges, 83–94; statistics of, 68–69; tracking system for, 60–72. *See also* Enrollment, Evaluation, Recruitment

Retention-driven marketing. *See* Marketing

Return potential, analysis of, 79

Rogers, B. H., 2, 61–72, 98, 99

St. John, E. P., 51, 60

Saint Louis Community College, retention-driven marketing at, 2, 74–81

SAT scores, analysis of, 15, 16, 66

Sauer, K., 17, 19

Scannell, J., 22, 32

Scholarship incentives, 52–54

Scholarships. *See* Financial aid, No-need scholarships

Simpson, D. B., 50, 60

Small colleges, evaluation at, 83–94, 96. *See also* Community colleges

Societal-political-economic perspective, 5

Software. *See* Computing

Southwest Missouri State University (SMSU), scholarships of, 50–51

Stockburger, D. W., 50, 60

Stockman, D., 47

Stop-out behavior, 75, 76–77

Strategic enrollment management, 8–9

Strategic planning, 1, 9–11, 18; and information systems, 26

Sudman, S., 11, 19

Surveys: analysis of, 39–43; development of, 35–38; targeted populations for, 38–39. *See also* Marketing

System design, 24–25. *See also* Information systems

Talmage, H., 5, 6, 19

Team approach, to evaluation systems, 26–27

Teeter, D. J., 69, 72

Telephone interviews, 38–39

Terenzini, P. T., 63, 72

Terkla, D. G., 2, 33–45, 96

Tichenor, R., 2, 73–81

Tinto, V., 49, 57, 60, 73–74, 81

Tracking system. *See* Decentralization, Longitudinal tracking system

Tufts University, admissions research in, 2, 33–45

Vesper, N., 26, 32

Voorhees, R. A., 52, 60

Werth, B., 95, 99

White, G. W., 50, 59

Wilcox, L., 2, 47–60, 96

Wisner, R. E., 17, 19

Wolfe, K. L., 70, 72

Woodward, C., 52, 60

Yield analysis, 15, 57, 89. *See also* Matrix

Zelenak, B., 50, 60

ORDERING INFORMATION

NEW DIRECTIONS FOR INSTITUTIONAL RESEARCH is a series of paperback books that provides planners and administrators in all types of academic institutions with guidelines in such areas as resource coordination, information analysis, program evaluation, and institutional management. Books in the series are published quarterly in Fall, Winter, Spring, and Summer and are available for purchase by subscription as well as by single copy.

SUBSCRIPTIONS for 1991 cost $45.00 for individuals (a savings of 20 percent over single-copy prices) and $60.00 for institutions, agencies, and libraries. Please do not send institutional checks for personal subscriptions. Standing orders are accepted.

SINGLE COPIES cost $13.95 when payment accompanies order. (California, New Jersey, New York, and Washington, D.C., residents please include appropriate sales tax.) Billed orders will be charged postage and handling.

DISCOUNTS FOR QUANTITY ORDERS are available. Please write to the address below for information.

ALL ORDERS must include either the name of an individual or an official purchase order number. Please submit your order as follows:
  Subscriptions: specify series and year subscription is to begin
  Single copies: include individual title code (such as IR1)

MAIL ALL ORDERS TO:
  Jossey-Bass Inc., Publishers
  350 Sansome Street
  San Francisco, California 94104

FOR SALES OUTSIDE OF THE UNITED STATES CONTACT:
  Maxwell Macmillan International Publishing Group
  866 Third Avenue
  New York, New York 10022

OTHER TITLES AVAILABLE IN THE
NEW DIRECTIONS FOR INSTITUTIONAL RESEARCH SERIES
Patrick T. Terenzini, Editor-in-Chief
Ellen Earle Chaffee, Associate Editor

IR69 Using National Data Bases, *Charles S. Lenth*
IR68 Assessing Academic Climates and Cultures, *William G. Tierney*
IR67 Adapting Strategic Planning to Campus Realities, *Frank A. Schmidtlein,
      Toby H. Milton*
IR66 Organizing Effective Institutional Research Offices, *Jennifer B. Presley*
IR65 The Effect of Assessment on Minority Student Participation, *Michael T. Nettles*
IR64 Enhancing Information Use in Decision Making, *Peter T. Ewell*
IR63 Managing Faculty Resources, *G. Gregory Lozier, Michael J. Dooris*
IR62 Studying the Impact of Student Aid on Institutions, *Robert H. Fenske*
IR61 Planning and Managing Higher Education Facilities, *Harvey H. Kaiser*
IR60 Alumni Research: Methods and Applications, *Gerlinda S. Melchiori*
IR59 Implementing Outcomes Assessment: Promise and Perils,
      Trudy W. Banta
IR58 Applying Statistics in Institutional Research, *Bernard D. Yancey*
IR57 Improving Teaching and Learning Through Research, *Joan S. Stark,
      Lisa A. Mets*
IR56 Evaluating Administrative Services and Programs, *Jon F. Wergin,
      Larry A. Braskamp*
IR55 Managing Information in Higher Education, *E. Michael Staman*
IR54 Designing and Using Market Research, *Robert S. Lay, Jean J. Endo*
IR53 Conducting Interinstitutional Comparisons, *Paul T. Brinkman*
IR52 Environmental Scanning for Strategic Leadership, *Patrick M. Callan*
IR51 Enhancing the Management of Fund Raising, *John A. Dunn, Jr.*
IR50 Measuring Faculty Research Performance, *John W. Creswell*
IR49 Applying Decision Support Systems in Higher Education,
      John Rohrbaugh, Anne Taylor McCartt
IR47 Assessing Educational Outcomes, *Peter T. Ewell*
IR39 Applying Methods and Techniques of Futures Research,
      James L. Morrison, William L. Renfro, Wayne I. Boucher
IR37 Using Research for Strategic Planning, *Norman P. Uhl*
IR36 Studying Student Attrition, *Ernest T. Pascarella*
IR35 Information Technology: Innovations and Applications,
      Bernard Sheehan
IR34 Qualitative Methods for Institutional Research, *Eileen Kuhns,
      S. V. Martorana*
IR33 Effective Planned Change Strategies, *G. Melvin Hipps*
IR32 Increasing the Use of Institutional Research, *Jack Lindquist*
IR31 Evaluation of Management and Planning Systems, *Nick L. Poulton*